Peer Tutoring *in* High School

Supporting Students With Disabilities in the General Education Classroom

REBECCA BROOKS
ELIZABETH CASTAGNERA

Foreword by Jacqueline Thousand

Solution Tree | Press

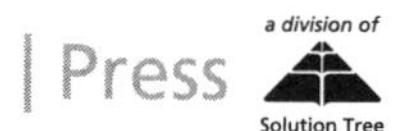

555 North Morton Street
Bloomington, IN 47404
800.733.6786 (toll free) / 812.336.7700
FAX: 812.336.7790

email: info@SolutionTree.com
SolutionTree.com

Visit **go.SolutionTree.com/specialneeds** to download the free reproducibles in this book.

Printed in the United States of America

Library of Congress Cataloging-in-Publication Data

Names: Brooks, Rebecca, 1974- author | Castagnera, Elizabeth author
Title: Peer tutoring in high school : supporting students with disabilities in the general education classroom / Rebecca Brooks, Elizabeth Castagnera ; foreword by Jacqueline Thousand.
Description: Bloomington, IN : Solution Tree Press, [2026] | Includes bibliographical references and index.
Identifiers: LCCN 2025053100 (print) | LCCN 2025053101 (ebook) | ISBN 9798893741117 paperback | ISBN 9798893741124 ebook
Subjects: LCSH: Students with disabilities--Services for | Peer teaching | Tutors and tutoring
Classification: LCC LC4015 .B746 2026 (print) | LCC LC4015 (ebook)
LC record available at https://lccn.loc.gov/2025053100
LC ebook record available at https://lccn.loc.gov/2025053101

Solution Tree
Cameron L. Rains, CEO
Edmund M. Ackerman, President

Solution Tree Press
Publisher: Kendra Slayton
Associate Publisher: Todd Brakke
Acquisitions Director: Hilary Goff
Editorial Director: Laurel Hecker
Art Director: Rian Anderson
Managing Editor: Sarah Ludwig
Copy Chief: Jessi Finn
Senior Production Editor: Tonya Maddox Cupp
Copy Editor: Anne Marie Watkins
Proofreader: Sarah Ludwig
Text and Cover Designer: Abigail Bowen
Content Development Specialist: Amy Rubenstein
Associate Editor: Elijah Oates
Editorial Assistant: Madison Chartier

Acknowledgments

This book is the result of the collective work of individuals who have a passion for including, supporting, and embracing all students, with and without disabilities. We collected the examples in this book over many years from several schools that experienced great success utilizing peer tutors as a form of support for effective inclusive school practices. We want to thank all of the educators, staff, students, and families who were part of the journey that contributed knowledge and resources for this book. It is our hope that readers will be able to take this information and utilize it in a way that is successful for students, teachers, and school communities.

—Rebecca and Elizabeth

Solution Tree Press would like to thank the following reviewers:

Joann Brewer
Special Education Teacher
Cane Ridge High School
Metropolitan Nashville Public Schools
Antioch, Tennessee

Jessica Clark
Special Education Teacher
Sanger High School
Sanger, California

Erik Hermansen
Principal
Fivay High School
Hudson, Florida

Brad Neuendorf
Principal
Lander Valley High School
Lander, Wyoming

Steven Weber
Assistant Principal
Rogers Heritage High School
Rogers, Arkansas

Visit **go.SolutionTree.com/specialneeds** to download the free reproducibles in this book.

Table of Contents

Reproducibles are in italics.

About the Authors

Rebecca Brooks, PhD, is an associate professor in the Special Education Combined Credential and Master's Degree Program at California State University San Marcos (CSUSM). She is the founder and director of the CSUSM Aspiring Scholars Program, an inclusive postsecondary education program for students with intellectual disabilities. Prior to joining the university faculty, she was a special educator for grades K–12, where she taught students included in general education classrooms. She has worked with individuals with disabilities in educational, recreational, vocational, and residential settings for more than thirty-five years.

Rebecca is a presenter and consultant in the United States in the areas of best practices for inclusive education, peer tutoring systems, and accommodations and modifications. She has written journal articles on peer tutoring and inclusive education and coauthored the book *Adapting Unstoppable Learning*. She has Multiple Subject and Education Specialist teaching credentials. Rebecca earned an associate's degree in developmental disabilities, a bachelor's degree in communicative disorders, a master's degree in education with an emphasis in special education, and a doctoral degree in education with a focus on social justice.

Elizabeth Castagnera, MA, is an educational consultant in assistive technology and leads a nonprofit organization that provides assistive technology to students transitioning out of high school programs. Previously, she dedicated thirty years to teaching special education at the high school level and developing peer tutoring programs. She also served as a lecturer in the special education departments at both San Diego State University and California State University San Marcos. Before her teaching career, Elizabeth worked in residential facilities for individuals with disabilities, committing herself to improving the quality of life and living conditions of others. She is a recognized presenter in the United States on topics such as inclusive education, peer tutoring systems, and accommodations and modifications. She has coauthored works in these areas as well, such as the article "Peer Supports and Inclusive Education: An Underutilized Resource" and the book *Deciding What to Teach and How to Teach It: Connecting Students Through Curriculum and Instruction*. Elizabeth has Multiple Subject and Education Specialist teaching credentials.

She holds an associate's degree in residential services from Grossmont College, as well as a bachelor's degree in liberal studies, a master's degree in special education, and a certificate in rehabilitation technology with a focus on assistive technology from San Diego State University.

To book Rebecca Brooks or Elizabeth Castagnera for professional development, contact pd@SolutionTree.com.

Foreword

BY JACQUELINE THOUSAND

Even in the best of economic times and in secondary schools with vast economic and human resources, it is unlikely for educators to say they have all the resources they need to educate every student in their classrooms in ways that are both rigorous and welcoming of students with diverse learning needs, including students with disabilities who have more intensive support needs. The reality is that many schools have lost or are at risk of losing precious resources, frustrating school personnel, families, and students alike. Fortunately, there is one resource that can never be taken away from educators—the students themselves. Yet, every day in many of our schools and classrooms, this precious resource is often underutilized. Many thanks to Rebecca Brooks and Elizabeth Castagnera for helping remedy this situation with the publication of *Peer Tutoring in High School: Supporting Students With Disabilities in the General Education Classroom*. Their book shows us how to capture the instructional talents and passions of the untapped resource of students while simultaneously structuring learning supports for classmates with disabilities so that high school classrooms can be genuinely inclusive.

Consider what high school students say at the end of the day when adults ask, "What did you do in school today?" Often, they reply, "Nothing!" While you might think this answer represents teenagers not wanting to share their day, interviews with students suggest that "nothing" accurately represents many students' perceptions of the relevance or meaningfulness of their day (Winthrop, Shoukry, & Nitkin, 2025). In contrast, in schools where educators deliberately empower students to provide instruction, make decisions, and advocate for themselves and their peers, students' answers are quite different (Villa, Thousand, & Nevin, 2010). They describe the meaningfulness of being part of the instructional team and making a difference in the learning of other classmates. What teacher and caregiver do not wish for this response? So, when human and fiscal resources are limited as they almost always are, why not explore the opportunity this book offers for tapping the most valuable educational resource of all—the students themselves?

I am a strong believer in the adage, "When you have a big enough *why*, you can overcome the biggest *how*." *Why* establish peer tutoring as a general education support for the inclusion of students with disabilities? Brooks and Castagnera clearly answer this question in the first three chapters of the book. Examining the multiple rationales for and decades of research demonstrating peer tutoring as a powerful evidence-based instructional strategy, they articulate the many benefits not only for the tutees but their tutors, teachers, and the greater educational community. Sharing real-life peer tutor partnership stories, they illustrate the life-altering and long-term social, academic, and personal outcomes of peer tutoring relationships.

Establishing a peer tutoring system is a novel and complex undertaking for anyone! So, *how* do educators go about the necessary tasks of organizing, implementing, monitoring, evaluating, and communicating the positive outcomes of a peer tutoring curriculum and instructional system? Brooks and Castagnera have considered, tested, and determined elegantly straightforward ways to accomplish all of these *how* tasks, sharing them in their evidenced-based, field-tested curriculum presented in the final eight chapters of the book. The instructional modules, student activities, and implementation tools provided here are expressly designed to make a peer tutoring system not only very *doable* but easily *adaptable* to any school's unique culture, population, and readiness to take on peer tutoring as an instructional innovation.

Once reading and discovering the whys and hows of this well-conceived curriculum for engaging high schoolers as coeducators, I anticipate that rather than asking, "*Why* engage teens as instructors and natural supporters of their classmates with disabilities?" the question you and other educators will ask is, "*Why not* collaborate with students as peer tutor co-instructors?" What is there to lose? We have the tools. Let's do it!

So, I invite you to read on. Deepen your understanding of the rationales and curricular elements for teaching and supporting youth to be instructors of and natural supports for their peers. Be that instructional leader whose engagement with and promotion of peer tutoring equips your high school students to give a most animated, empowered, purpose-filled, and passionate answer to the age-old question, "What did you do in school today?"

Introduction

Whoever teaches learns in the act of teaching, and whoever learns teaches in the act of learning.

—PAULO FREIRE

Inclusive education allows all students the opportunity to learn together, recognizing and valuing both their similarities and differences. *Inclusive education*—based on the principle that all students have the right to access an equitable education—consists of teaching students with disabilities alongside their same-age peers in general education classrooms. By providing students with disabilities the appropriate supports and services to address their individualized needs, educators can successfully include them with their peers without disabilities. This ensures their access to general education curricula, rather than being taught in separate settings. The foundation of this approach is that all people are respected and differences are valued—not just tolerated. When schools implement inclusive practices, they do so based on the benefits they offer students with disabilities, the invaluable lessons they provide to all students, and the spirit of acceptance they represent in a school community.

Peer tutoring is a very effective—though often underused—way that schools can support students with disabilities in general education classes and promote an inclusive culture. Peer supports are effective at all ages (Collins, Lo, Haughney, & Park, 2021; Mauer & Swanson, 2025; Morgan, Kim, & Fienup, 2020; Wilt & Morningstar, 2020). These supports benefit the following groups of people, and we discuss their benefits in chapter 1.

- The tutees (Carter et al., 2017; Carter, Steinbrenner, & Hall, 2019; Haas, Vannest, Fuller, & Ganz, 2022; Huber & Carter, 2023; Malone, Fodor, & Hollingshead, 2019; Shukla, Kennedy, & Cushing, 1998, 1999; Staub, Spaulding, Peck, Gallucci, & Schwartz, 1996)

- The tutors (Bond, 2001; Brooks, 2014; Cushing & Kennedy, 1997; Owen-DeSchryver, Ziegler, Matthews, Mayberry, & Carter, 2024; Schaefer, Cannella-Malone, & Carter, 2016; Travers & Carter, 2022a)
- The educators (Klavina & Block, 2008; Thompson, 2011)
- The community at large (Brooks, 2014; Travers & Carter, 2022a)

Well-developed peer tutoring programs allow schools to successfully include students with disabilities in general education classes. Without the individualized, one-to-one support these programs provide, many students with disabilities would be unable to attend the general education classrooms, and, even if they did attend, they might be unable to fully participate without a peer tutor. For example, we worked at one high school in Southern California that had sixteen students with intellectual and developmental disabilities. These students had one special educator and four paraprofessionals assigned to their classroom. Clearly, there were not enough adults to provide each of these students the one-to-one support they needed to participate in the general education classrooms. In fact, many of the students didn't need or want an adult going with them to all of their classes. They preferred peer support.

Due to the immense need for additional support, we developed a peer tutoring elective course. The first semester, sixteen students enrolled in the course. The enrollment numbers increased each semester, quickly reaching a semester total of 125 peer tutors. This allowed each student with a disability to have a different peer tutor for each period of the school day. In cases where a student required a paraprofessional, the student was also assigned a peer tutor to reap the benefits of peer support. As a result of the course, all students received the personal support they needed to participate in a wide range of learning opportunities and robust activities in general education settings with their peers.

Schools that are currently struggling to meet the needs of students in general education settings are likely to benefit from implementing peer supports. If a student can benefit from having the support of a peer tutor, it is essential that we consider it an option. Peer tutor support can truly impact a student's access to an equitable education. Therefore, having such a support system available at school sites is a critical component to creating an effective inclusive school setting. Not only are peer tutors vital personal supports, but they can also provide assistance in other areas, including curricular adaptations and instructional and assistive technology.

ABOUT THIS BOOK

This book serves as a practical, easy-to-use resource for grades 9–12 general and special educators. It is filled with creative, innovative strategies for implementing a peer support system that fosters inclusive educational opportunities. We outline for you how, with the support of administrators, you can develop a robust peer tutoring course for high schools, complete with course curriculum and organizational systems to ensure smooth program implementation. You'll gain a deep understanding of the roles and responsibilities of peer tutors: who they are, what they do, and how they significantly impact inclusive education. We also share mutual benefits for tutors and tutees and the ways peer tutoring fosters increased academic skill development, social opportunities, and personal development. We explain the benefits of peer tutoring and provide concrete steps and tools, including reproducible materials, to help you establish and implement (or refine) an effective peer tutoring system at your school.

Keep in mind that, though we provide a tried-and-true course description, a peer tutoring course will look different from school to school. A course will evolve based on students' needs, your school's dynamics, and current educational issues. The course will also look different from year to year because it should be individualized to address the students' and school's needs. We also provide suggestions and examples to help you generate your own ideas. Finally, recognize that designing and implementing a course like the one we describe in this book does not happen overnight.

Set aside planning time, during either the summer or the previous school year, for organizing the program launch. The first year of implementation will have the fewest students enrolled due to the course being new and unfamiliar. However, with good advertisement throughout the first year and the program's growing popularity, the number of peer tutors often increases rapidly. Typically, by the second year, a peer tutoring program will have solid numbers and begin to run smoothly, with each subsequent year continuing to grow and become more developed.

While this book focuses on peer tutoring at the high school level, a peer tutoring course can also be created and implemented at middle schools in very similar ways. However, middle school schedules may not be designed to offer elective courses each period or block of the school day, which can make it challenging to provide peer tutor support throughout the entire day. This is where creativity becomes essential.

Peer support is also a valuable resource in elementary schools. Obviously, an elementary school would not implement peer support in the form of a course students enroll in. Rather, it would consist of organized planning and scheduling in the elementary classroom, thus allowing the entire class to learn the skills needed to effectively support another student, whether with individual assignments or during collaborative group learning activities. You could pair students on a rotating basis. An additional option is to take advantage of cross-age peer tutoring through collaboration with other grade levels. For example, fifth graders can work with first graders. These are a few ways you can implement peer support at the elementary school level.

HOW THIS BOOK IS ORGANIZED

The elements in this book are organized into two parts. Part 1 (chapters 1–3) provides the background for the peer tutoring course, and part 2 (chapters 4–11) provides the curriculum.

- Chapter 1 explains how the law intersects with a peer tutoring course (especially in terms of privacy) and what components the triangle of support contains. That triangle will help you visualize the wide range of supplementary aids and services that peer tutors can provide. You will also explore research about the benefits that everyone—tutees, tutors, teachers, and communities at large—receives from peer tutors.
- Chapter 2 explains what is required of a student to be a peer tutor and provides snapshots of real peer tutors. Additionally, this chapter covers the types of support tutors can be tasked with. Here, you get an idea of how students work together and how tutors can assist students with disabilities by reading aloud to them; taking notes for them; keeping them on task; helping them record, complete, and turn in assignments; and more.
- Chapter 3 gives step-by-step instructions for creating a peer tutoring course, from administrative support to course development to advertisement of the course to students and families. Development includes details such as choosing a teacher of record and possible prerequisites, as well as deciding curriculum and assessment. In addition, we explain how to pair students, encourage communication, create an organization system, and address attendance so you can fully develop and plan for as much as possible.
- Chapter 4 begins part 2, which lays out the curriculum structure, training, activities, and materials that peer tutors need over the course of seven sessions. We dive into session one, which covers inclusive education, the expectations for peer tutors, and the course-long digital portfolio project.
- Chapter 5 is about session two, during which tutors learn about different helpful strategies and levels of prompting when working with their tutee. This chapter explains curriculum accessibility via adaptations (modifications and accommodations).
- Chapter 6 covers session three, which focuses on the importance of increasing tutors' communication skills. We discuss strategies that peer tutors can implement and their role in teaching these very important skills. We also recommend a visit from a speech-language pathologist (SLP), a professional many students with disabilities are familiar with.

- Chapter 7 describes session four, where students in the peer tutoring course learn about how they can help facilitate social inclusion. Inclusion is one of the big benefits that research bears out for students with disabilities, so we include multiple activities in this chapter to help peer tutors cultivate empathy for students with disabilities and comprehend the importance of social inclusion.
- Chapter 8 focuses on the book talk assignment, which is not restricted to session five. With this project, students gain insight into the perspectives of individuals with disabilities by reading a novel whose main character has a disability.
- Chapter 9 details session six, where students dig into a research project. Perhaps more than any other activity or assignment in the course, this one is interdisciplinary. During the project, they choose a specific disability or disability-related topic to research (including, but not limited to, inclusive education itself), and then they write about it.
- Chapter 10 covers session seven, where students will present the digital portfolio project that they worked on throughout the course. These presentations include the assignments and prompt responses they completed throughout the course, with the highlight potentially being their written responses to two final prompts asking them to reflect on their time as tutors and to provide realia and artifacts from their time with the student they tutored.
- Chapter 11 provides alternatives to holding formalized training sessions throughout the school year. For schools that choose not to do the training sessions outlined in chapters 4–10, we offer sample assignments and activities that can function as homework.
- In the epilogue, we share our thoughts on peer tutoring's potential and future.

We provide reproducible resources throughout the book to make it easy for teachers to implement the tools and activities we describe in each chapter. Also, throughout the book, you will read quotes from students who have participated in peer tutoring programs and will gain insight through frequently asked questions.

Part 1

PREPARING A PEER TUTORING COURSE

This part helps you understand what is involved in a peer tutoring course, how to propose a course to your administrator, and how to create the course.

- **Chapter 1:** Explains legalities, the triangle of support, and the benefits of peer tutors
- **Chapter 2:** Describes the peer tutor role and provides snapshots of real peer tutors
- **Chapter 3:** Gives step-by-step instructions and guidance for creating a peer tutoring course, including curriculum development and administrative support

CHAPTER 1

Reasons That Peer Tutors Are a Good Idea

The following quote provides insight into how students with intellectual and developmental disabilities often feel about being supported by a paraprofessional (an employed adult aide) in their classroom setting throughout their educational career:

> I was kind of getting embarrassed because I always had, like a mother right there. People were like looking at me and stuff, and saying, "Why do you always have this person with you who is twice as old as you?" (Broer, Doyle, & Giangreco, 2005, p. 420)

Although paraprofessionals are an incredible option for students in need of one-to-one support, it is important to recognize the impact that adult support can have on students' social connections and sense of belonging.

While educators and paraprofessionals provide immense support to students, schools don't have enough adult staff to give one-to-one assistance to all students who could benefit from it, nor do students always require it. In addition, paraprofessional support can negatively affect students' self-perceptions and their relationships with their classroom peers (Broer et al., 2005). The use of peers, when implemented in structured support systems, actually increases social interaction with peers for students with disabilities (van der Meulen, Granizo, & del Barrio, 2021). Therefore, peers can be an optimal option, offering numerous benefits for both the tutor and tutee.

Finally, it is important to note that while employed adult aides have various titles across districts—*paraprofessionals*, *instructional aides*, *paraeducators*, *teaching assistants*, and more—we refer to any employed adult aide supporting students with disabilities as a *paraprofessional* in this book.

Students with disabilities often require varying levels of support to access general education curricula, participate in activities, and be meaningfully included in their classrooms. While this support is required by law, you can deliver it in numerous ways. Due to its wide range of benefits and successes, peer tutoring is a valuable and effective support strategy that should be considered as a valid option. The following sections discuss how the law intersects with a peer tutoring course, what the triangle of support contains, and what the benefits of peer tutoring are.

THE LAW

The Individuals With Disabilities Education Act (IDEA, 2004), originally known as the Education for All Handicapped Children Act of 1975, mandates that children with disabilities be provided a *free appropriate public education* (FAPE) in the *least restrictive environment.* Since then, the law has been reauthorized many times to clarify the meaning of *least restrictive environment.* Additionally, reauthorizations have established criteria for educating a student in an environment outside of the general education classroom.

Section 1412(a)(5) of IDEA (2004) defines *least restrictive environment* as follows:

> Special classes, separate schooling, or other removal of children with disabilities from the regular educational environment occurs only when the nature or severity of the disability of a child is such that education in regular classes with the use of supplementary aids and services cannot be achieved satisfactorily.

Educators now recognize that inclusive education is no longer just a philosophy that some believe to be sound. Rather, it is a law that all U.S. schools must comply with. After reviewing evidence from more than 280 studies conducted in twenty-five countries, researchers find:

> [There is] consistent evidence that inclusive educational settings—those in which children with disabilities are educated alongside their non-disabled peers—can confer substantial short- and long-term benefits for children's cognitive and social development. . . . The research evidence also suggests that . . . inclusion can have important positive benefits for all students. . . . Effectively including a student with a disability requires teachers and school administrators to develop a better understanding of the individual strengths and needs of every student. (Hehir et al., 2016, p. 26)

The challenge for educators lies in how to support students in general education classrooms so that all students reach their highest potential while working within the confines of ever-diminishing resources. Peer tutoring is one accessible and free resource that can provide this support.

THE TRIANGLE OF SUPPORT

The wide range of supplementary aids and services that students can receive are easily visualized as three separate areas of support, often referred to as the *triangle of support* (Castagnera, Fisher, Rodifer, Sax, & Frey, 2003). See figure 1.1 for a visualization of this triangle.

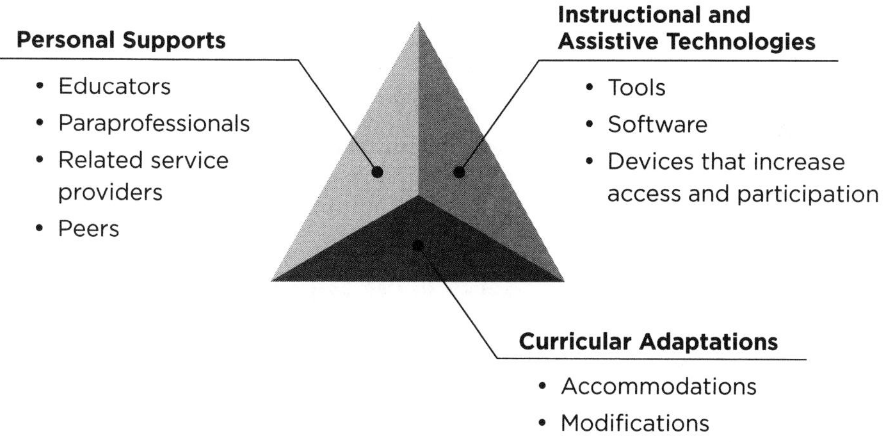

Source: Castagnera et al., 2003. Adapted with permission.

Figure 1.1: *The triangle of support.*

For many students, receiving support in these three areas is critical to their educational success. For students with disabilities to truly have access to—and effectively participate in—general education classes, some will require support in one or more of these areas. If a student is not successful in their classes or if it appears they are unable to be included in a general education classroom, educators should explore the triangle of support to ensure assistance in these areas is offered.

Personal Supports

Personal support refers to any person providing assistance to a student, such as educators, paraprofessionals or related service providers, and yes, you guessed it, peer tutors! In fact, one of the most readily available resources for supporting students in their classes is other students. Although there are times when using paraprofessionals to assist individual students is appropriate, in many cases, using peer tutors is not only more cost effective but more beneficial for the tutored student, both academically and socially (Haas et al., 2022; Hehir et al., 2016; Huber & Carter, 2023). Regardless of how you implement it, the outcomes are positive for students both with and without disabilities when students are given the opportunity to provide support to one another (Biggs, Carter, & Gustafson, 2017; Carter et al., 2017, 2019; Haas et al., 2022; Huber & Carter, 2023; Longwill & Kleinert, 1998; Travers & Carter, 2022a).

The personal support that originates in a peer tutoring program can be especially important to adolescents, who, during this developmental age, often highly value connections with their peers. As we mentioned, the presence of an adult can sometimes be off-putting for students, who may be reluctant to spend time in the supervising company of an adult staff member, such as a paraprofessional. While we deliberately clarify that a peer tutoring course is not a friendship program, we recognize the value of offering opportunities for students to interact, which in turn has the potential to foster natural, meaningful relationships.

Can support from an adult (such as a paraprofessional) be faded so a peer tutor can assist the student?

Yes. Many students can gradually decrease their need for adult support and can often become successful with peer tutors instead. The peer tutors can go to class with the paraprofessional, and the paraprofessional can slowly fade their support. For some students, a paraprofessional will always be necessary due to a variety of reasons, such as medical needs. The paraprofessional can always monitor the student from the back of the classroom while the peer tutor provides the direct support. The paraprofessional may be able to assist other students, as well, while continuing to observe their assigned student.

Can support from a peer tutor be faded?

Yes. The ultimate goal is for students to become as independent as possible. If a student is able to attend all or part of any of their classes on their own, then support from the peer tutor is slowly faded. We have had students request an Individualized Education Program (IEP) goal to fade peer tutor assistance and attend a class independently.

How do parents and guardians tend to feel about peer tutors?

Families have shared positive views about peer tutors. Usually, they are excited for their child to have additional support, and they see the many benefits of that support coming from a peer. For some, this may be the first time their child has been given the option of peer support. That said, some parents or caregivers may be hesitant in the beginning if this type of support is new to them. However, when families are given the opportunity to meet their child's peer tutor, they often feel reassured. This can occur during a family day or a scheduled classroom visit. Some parents or guardians have certain requests, such as a male or female peer tutor, which should be honored.

In addition to having a well-developed peer tutoring program, educators should also consider natural forms of supporting students with disabilities by using the students already in their classes. Students who are enrolled in the same class and able to provide support to one another are often called *natural supports*. This is an important component of any educational program. Some educators choose to create and implement an organized support system in their classroom where they pair a different set of students each day, as needed. Other teachers might simply create an environment that regularly embeds cooperative learning opportunities where all students can learn and support one another. When students with and without disabilities participate in cooperative learning, it positively impacts peer relationships, peer support, and classroom engagement (Van Ryzin, Murray, & Roseth, 2024). Natural support systems are invaluable and should be implemented when possible.

Curricular Adaptations

While peer tutors are considered personal supports in the triangle of support, *curricular adaptations*, defined as changes made to the curriculum, encompass all accommodations and modifications.

While educators must consider the following questions for all their students, they pay particular attention to students receiving accommodations or modifications per their Individualized Education Program.

- **Does the student have the means to access the curriculum?** For students to learn the content and participate in classroom activities, they must be able to access what is provided to them, whether it be the instructions, reading materials, an activity handout, or a homework assignment.
- **Does the student have the means to effectively demonstrate their learning?** For students to effectively show what they have learned and be assessed equitably, they must receive assessment formats that remove barriers and accurately reflect their knowledge.

Accommodations

When students need support accessing the curriculum, the most common way to do so is through curricular *accommodations*. With accommodations, teachers change how they deliver content or how the student demonstrates their mastery of the content. Accommodations do not change any standards, and students learn the same content; however, they may receive the information in a different format. For example, providing a student with a book in braille or in audio format is an accommodation, as it only changes the way the information is delivered to the student; it does not change what the student is expected to learn. In addition, if the student is asked to answer an open-ended question but is given an accommodation of using a graphic organizer or speech-to-text tool, what the student is expected to demonstrate does not change. Rather, what changes is how the student shows their knowledge of the content.

Modifications

Due to differences in cognitive abilities, sometimes it becomes necessary to adapt the content taught or change the task assigned in order for the student to access it and participate. Therefore, some students may need curricular *modifications*. This results in a change to the content or task itself and, potentially, the standard. For example, if students are asked to read a chapter in a textbook and answer open-ended comprehension questions, a student who requires modifications may be provided with a one-page summary of the chapter that highlights several of the chapter's key points and be asked to answer multiple-choice questions about what they read.

So how does this relate to peer tutors? Peer tutors do not design curricular accommodations and modifications; the general and special educators design and provide them. The role of the peer tutor is to support the student in engaging with the accessible curriculum provided to them in a general education classroom. With that said, in our experience, peer tutors consistently shine as a source of creativity for effective accommodations and modifications, and they can be encouraged to share their ideas with both the special and general educators. In addition, they often possess great insight into what works and what doesn't from their own perspectives as a student and their personal connections with the students they support.

Instructional and Assistive Technology

Instructional and assistive technology provides endless opportunities for students as technology continually advances. There are some important distinctions between instructional technology and assistive technology. *Instructional technology* enhances teaching and learning and is often used in educational settings to ensure students have access to curricula and educational activities. *Assistive technology* is often defined as supports that are designed for individuals with disabilities to aid in their participation in activities, promoting inclusivity and independence. Obviously, there can be some overlap. What is important is that technological supports are regularly explored and provided to students as needed.

- Low-tech supports can be something as simple as a pencil grip, highlighter, or graphic organizer.
- Mid-tech supports can include audiobooks or magnifiers.
- High-tech supports include augmentative and alternative communication devices and speech-to-text applications.

Many instructional and assistive technology options are overlooked as possible supports for students, especially high-tech supports. A possible reason for this may be that school personnel make assumptions that the technology is unattainable due to the cost. However, state, provincial, and federal legislation can support the school's acquisition of assistive technology. If the student's IEP determines a need for a certain type of assistive technology, then schools must provide it for the student at no cost to the family. Therefore, consider assistive technology as a viable support for students with disabilities in the general education classroom.

As with providing curricular support, the peer tutor's responsibility is at the implementation level. This can include modeling and supporting the use of technology, which is especially important for students who are learning how to use augmentative and alternative communication devices. Because peer tutors are often observing students using technology, they can be invaluable to students' support systems. For example, peer tutors often assist with troubleshooting technology when it malfunctions by informing educators about possible glitches, allowing staff to address problems as soon as possible. In other cases, peer tutors can communicate to educators when they think a specialized piece of equipment might be necessary for a future class activity. The peer tutor's role can be to support the student while they learn to use new assistive technology, which helps ensure the student has access to curricula and can actively participate in learning activities.

Educators who oversee peer tutors are responsible for training them on the various instructional and assistive technologies in use, as well as in effective strategies for supporting students who use them. In addition, course creators can seamlessly incorporate an overview of instructional and assistive technology into tutor training sessions and tailor content to the specific technologies implemented at the school.

As we mentioned, all three areas of the triangle of support are essential to inclusive practices. When assessing the current needs of students in general education classrooms, it's important to ensure that supports are explored in all three areas: (1) personal supports, (2) curricular adaptations, and (3) instructional and assistive technologies. If any of these three areas has unmet needs, a student's potential for success may be lowered (Fernández-Batanero, Montenegro-Rueda, Fernández-Cerero, & García-Martínez, 2022; Gee, Ryndak, Fisher, & Walker, 2024; Van Ryzin et al., 2024). The great news is that with intention in these areas, students can receive the support they need and can find success in their education!

BENEFITS OF PEER TUTORING

As you've seen throughout this chapter, peer tutors are underused resources that provide research-backed benefits. With some planning and organizing, a successful peer tutoring system can easily be implemented at no cost. In addition, the immense benefits for both peer tutors and the students receiving this support cannot be overlooked. Everyone benefits from peer tutoring systems, including students, staff, and the school community.

Benefits for Students With Disabilities

Students with disabilities accessing peer supports receive many benefits, both academic and social. Students with disabilities receiving peer supports in general education classrooms demonstrate increased academic engagement and skill acquisition (Carter et al., 2016, 2017, 2019; Haas et al., 2022; Huber & Carter, 2023; Malone et al., 2019; Shukla et al., 1998, 1999; Staub et al., 1996). For example, studies of peer-mediated academic instruction for students with autism show moderate engagement effects, and studies of academic skill acquisition or reading comprehension demonstrate large effects (Haas et al., 2022). In addition, students who receive peer supports engage more academically and make greater gains in social-skills acquisition compared to students who only receive adult support (Carter et al., 2016).

Students with disabilities benefit from positive role models. Peer tutors demonstrate both the academic and social skills that many students try to gain. Peer tutors can display to all students the behaviors and skills needed to be an engaged, successful student who includes all their peers. Many times, students want to attend on-campus activities, clubs, or events but may feel uncomfortable doing so alone, may not know how to navigate these activities, or may require one-to-one support to participate. Again, through the course we provide in this book, you can pair students so that all can attend and actively participate in any campus event!

Peer support expands the social network for students with disabilities (Biggs et al., 2017; Brock & Huber, 2017; Carter et al., 2016). Peer support increases the number of social interactions among students with and without disabilities in general education classrooms (Brock & Huber, 2017). In addition, students who use assistive technology to communicate demonstrate increased peer interactions when provided peer support (Biggs et al., 2017).

Peer support can increase the odds of students with significant disabilities being included in general education classrooms (Agran et al., 2020; Thompson et al., 2020). Research finds that these students are often excluded from general education classrooms, not because of their learning needs but because of other factors, such as belief systems, teacher experience, and a lack of resources (Agran et al., 2020). Educators identify time and resource constraints and a lack of personnel as the most common barriers to including students with intellectual disabilities in general education classrooms (Thompson et al., 2020). Peer support increases the number of students who can access one-to-one support in general education classrooms and allows students to receive immediate support, rather than having to wait until an educator is available.

I have witnessed my son excel in all areas of academics since having peer tutor support that has allowed [him] to not only be included in a general education class but have the one-to-one support he needed to truly participate in the learning activities.

—Parent of a child receiving peer tutor support

The gains are not just academic; they are broadly social. While school focuses on academics, personal K–12 experiences often evoke memories of friendships for all students. Students with disabilities who are paired with a peer tutor have increased opportunities to develop social skills, as well as interact and build relationships with peers (Brock & Huber, 2017; Carter et al., 2017; Carter, Sisco, Melekoglu, & Kurkowski, 2007; Huber & Carter, 2023; Shukla et al., 1998, 1999; Staub et al., 1996). The more opportunities students have to meet one another and spend time together, the more relationships they build. While many of these relationships will continue as school acquaintances, some will develop into deeper, long-lasting friendships.

Benefits for Peer Tutors

Students serving as peer tutors benefit immensely from their experience in this role. Peer tutors increase their understanding of and respect for students with a wide range of individual differences (Brooks, 2014; Travers & Carter, 2022a, 2022c). The largest impact that providing support to students with intellectual and developmental disabilities has on peer tutors is a positive change in their views of people with disabilities (Travers & Carter, 2022a). Not only are students' understanding of and respect for individual differences positively impacted *while* they serve as peer tutors, but these positive impacts remain for many years following the peer tutoring experience, which supports the idea that long-term benefits do exist (Brooks, 2014).

Students take these experiences into adulthood. Years after their experiences, former peer tutors are more likely to feel comfortable with people with disabilities, whether they work alongside or hire a person with a disability, have a neighbor with a disability, or assist a person with a disability (Brooks, 2014).

By holding students accountable for their daily impact and requiring them to complete reflective tasks (such as journal entries), educators instill personal responsibility, intrapersonal development, and personal development (Staub et al., 1996; Travers & Carter, 2022a, 2022c). As peer tutors, students also learn valuable teaching techniques as they support students with a wide range of learning needs. They develop the ability to problem-solve and be creative. Communication and interpersonal skills increase through peer tutoring (Travers & Carter, 2022c), which are useful as they continue their own learning journeys and later begin careers.

While serving as peer tutors, these students take on the responsibility of effectively communicating with special educators, general educators, paraprofessionals, and other school staff members in a timely manner. Through this experience, peer tutors become more comfortable speaking with adults and authority figures (Travers & Carter, 2022a). They also learn the skills to effectively communicate with the students they support, which can include understanding the concepts of behavior as communication or the use of augmentative and alternative communication systems.

I supported him to complete his work in his class. I always remembered to be patient. Since I became his peer tutor, he learned so much and his grade increased a lot. The teacher even noticed that with my support he was taking notes correctly and his homework was improving.

—Peer tutor

While the focus of school is often thought to be learning content, it is also making connections with others. As mentioned, when students share what they remember most about school, their responses often are filled with social experiences. As a peer tutor, this opportunity is expanded even further, as students are given the unique opportunity to support another student one to one, providing them with the space to build peer relationships (Schaefer et al., 2016; Travers & Carter, 2022a). Sometimes these relationships turn into friendships, though not always. Either way is OK.

But having this opportunity with peers—especially those they may not have otherwise connected with—enhances the lives of both individuals. The more people students can interact with, the more they can build on their capacity to understand and connect with others, as well as recognize and appreciate the diverse world we live in. Empathy is associated with enhanced social connections and may be linked to increased well-being in others (Morelli, Lieberman, & Zaki, 2015). Peer relations, in the context of cooperative learning, contribute to the development of *affective empathy* (understanding the emotional states of others); in turn, they also reduce bullying over time, positively impacting the entire school community (Van Ryzin & Roseth, 2022).

This role also provides the peer tutor with an opportunity to increase their knowledge in and engagement with course content, which is an academic benefit often not thought about nor highlighted (Bond, 2001; Cushing & Kennedy, 1997; Owen-DeSchryver et al., 2024; Schaefer et al., 2016). They also demonstrate academic growth in the areas they are tutoring in and find tutoring to be a beneficial learning opportunity (Bond, 2001). Some peer tutors self-report learning more academically in a class where they serve as a peer tutor than in one where they are enrolled as a student themselves. Most students feel that serving as a peer tutor better prepares them academically for future classes.

Grade point averages significantly increase, and absences decrease, for peers who actively support schoolmates with autism and other developmental disabilities (Owen-DeSchryver et al., 2024). Along with these benefits is a tremendous increase in the self-esteem of peer tutors who struggle in their own learning yet flourish as peer tutors. When their own grades improve, these peer tutors attribute this success to the experience of teaching others (Bond, 2001). By teaching others—which requires peer tutors to develop an understanding of the material, break it down, and then explain it in their own words—peer tutors are learning themselves!

Peer tutors are exposed to a wide variety of insights into numerous fields. They are given the opportunity to observe general educators, special educators, paraprofessionals, counselors, physical therapists, occupational therapists, mobility specialists, speech-language pathologists—the list goes on. With such a wide range of professionals to interact with, peer tutors may develop interests in careers they may not have thought about (Brooks, 2014; Travers & Carter, 2022a).

Benefits for Educators

Peer tutors also provide a great deal of support to both general and special educators. Peer tutors assist not only educators (by providing one-to-one support to their assigned students) but also any student in class as needed. In addition, you can properly train peer tutors and supervise them as they assist in the simple creation or implementation of curricular accommodations and modifications. These adaptations are often simple (enlarging a font or adding visual supports, for instance) and sometimes incredibly time consuming, so having an extra set of hands, along with new ideas, can be of tremendous support to educators.

Peer tutoring systems can offer educators and staff the gift of more time. By providing one-to-one support or assisting with curricular adaptations, peer tutors give educators more time to facilitate whole-group instruction, supervise small-group work, provide individualized support to more students, and ensure the implementation of curricular modifications and accommodations. The need for teacher interactions decreases as peer support increases for students with disabilities (Klavina & Block, 2008). With peer tutoring, schools free up much-needed time for the teacher while ensuring students with disabilities receive the one-to-one support they need to be successful.

Additional benefits for educators are the academic, behavioral, and social-emotional outcomes that result from reduced bullying (Van Ryzin & Roseth, 2022). Any bullying reduction will positively impact both educators and students. Educators perceive peer tutoring as a beneficial teaching strategy, and students respond more positively to peers than to teachers due to possible feelings of intimidation by an adult (Thompson, 2011). Some students feel more comfortable seeking guidance from their peers.

A systematic review of the literature indicates that peer-mediated interventions hold promise to replace the need to use adults as supports or to replace educators' extensive modifications (Mahoney, 2023). It is important to note that peer tutors can also supplement adult support, with the idea that adult support may be faded when appropriate. When fading adult support, you can increase peer support. As we mentioned, peer support (compared to exclusive paraprofessional support) increases social interactions, academic engagement, and friendship development in general education settings (Carter et al., 2016).

Benefits for the School Community

The entire school community can benefit greatly from an effective peer tutoring program. When there is a peer tutoring program offered at a school site, students, staff, and faculty take an active role in continuously recognizing the needs of students and providing peer assistance. Instead of relying solely on adults to give guidance, faculty and staff can encourage students to seek support from one another. Once peer tutors are trained to respond to the needs of the student they support, they can use this skill set to help any of their peers, with or without a disability. Peer tutoring builds a culture of support across the campus as a whole as trained peer tutors become exceptional models for others. This creates a supportive, inclusive school environment.

Peer tutoring also has the potential to increase students' acceptance of differing learning abilities and styles, thereby reducing stereotyping, bullying behaviors, and prejudicial attitudes. Educators report that peer tutoring creates an atmosphere of warmth within their classrooms, resulting in a greater sense of community with their students (Thompson, 2011). An inclusive, supportive classroom culture can spread across the campus and then extend to the surrounding community, continuing to influence students well into the future.

The students who have been taught in inclusive classrooms, where supporting other students is the norm, will become the future lawmakers, teachers, doctors, business owners, voters, and citizens who will make community and business decisions that affect everyone, including people with differing learning and support needs. The experiences students have had, whether as peer tutors themselves or as witnesses, can affect how they choose to treat people with disabilities in the future, since peer tutors report a positive change in attitudes and increased empathy toward peers with disabilities (Schaefer et al., 2016; Travers & Carter, 2022c). Therefore, students will hopefully be an active part in creating a society that supports all individuals.

Students enrolled in a peer tutoring course are statistically more likely to choose a university major in teaching, health sciences, or human services (Brooks, 2014). There is a scarcity of professionals in these related fields, especially those working with individuals with disabilities. The American Network of Community Options and Resources (ANCOR, 2025) reported moderate to severe staffing shortages in 2024–2025 for community-based providers of intellectual and developmental disabilities services, with 62 percent of providers not accepting patients due to insufficient staff. Shortages in special education teachers and essential support staff (including related service providers) are substantially high, which drastically impacts the education of students with disabilities (U.S. Commission on Civil Rights, 2025).

SUMMARY

This chapter explored what peer tutors are and how they can effectively support students with disabilities in inclusive classroom settings. It also highlighted the many benefits of peer tutoring—not only for students with disabilities but also for peer tutors, educators, and the broader school community.

CHAPTER 2

Overview of the Peer Tutor Role

As general educators, special educators, and administrators learn about the possibilities and benefits of implementing a peer tutoring course in their school, it is essential that they clearly understand who peer tutors are, what their responsibilities entail, and how the program benefits the entire school community. Schools may consider establishing a peer tutoring course for several reasons, including fostering a more inclusive school culture by expanding inclusive educational opportunities, providing a support system for students with disabilities in general education classrooms, and promoting meaningful academic and social growth for both students with disabilities and those serving as peer tutors.

This chapter provides educators and administrators with a clear overview of the peer tutor's role and how peer tutoring can support the inclusion of students with disabilities in general education classrooms. Understanding the wide variety of academic and social supports peer tutors can provide will allow educators to thoughtfully design a peer tutor course that meets the unique needs of their students and school site. Real-life accounts from students who have participated as tutors or tutees are included to illustrate the effectiveness of peers providing support. These firsthand perspectives demonstrate how peer tutoring can facilitate meaningful relationships, enhance school experiences, and promote more inclusive and collaborative school environments.

WHO PEER TUTORS ARE

Peer tutors are high school students who are enrolled in a peer tutoring course that earns elective credits. Tutors provide support to students with disabilities in a general education classroom during their school day. This course trains students on how to be an effective peer tutor, with a curriculum that addresses a wide range of academic, social, and emotional needs of students with disabilities. It is important to note that the peer tutoring course is considered an elective, and enrollees receive the same number of credits as any other elective course offered at your school. While open to any student in any grade, the peer tutoring course is highly recommended for students seeking a future in areas such as health sciences, human development, psychology, social work, education, physical therapy, occupational therapy, speech and language services, medicine, counseling, and other related fields.

While peer tutors may be assigned to work with a *group* of students, they are most often paired with one student with a disability to provide one-to-one support in a general education classroom. They can provide a wide range of assistance in almost any class, based on the student's individual needs, and can support student access to extracurricular activities.

Wow . . . it's amazing how a class that I only took for one year in high school has had more of a significant impact on my life than any other class I have taken in all four years.

—Peer tutor

Peer tutors attend seven training sessions provided by a special education teacher or other staff member knowledgeable of the scheduled topics. The reproducible "Peer Tutor Training Sessions at a Glance" (page 34) offers a bird's-eye view of all the lesson plans. These training sessions can occur anytime throughout the school year. However, we recommend that you introduce the following topics earlier in the school year. Doing so helps ensure that students receive the necessary training as close to the beginning of the school year or semester as possible (ideally within the first several weeks) so they have the skill set to provide adequate support as soon as possible.

- Inclusive education
- Peer tutor expectations
- Support strategies

The training sessions equip peer tutors with support strategies and tools to be effective and responsible. The curriculum detailed in part 2 for the peer tutoring course training sessions consists of education in the following areas: inclusive education, peer tutor expectations, support strategies and curriculum accessibility, communication skills, and the facilitation of social inclusion.

All students have the potential to become excellent peer tutors. Students do not need to excel academically themselves to learn how to effectively support another student in their learning journey. A student's desire to help another student or create an inclusive school culture matters more than their grades on a report card.

Read further to learn who peer tutors are, what they do, and what does not disqualify someone from being a good tutor, as well as to hear from real students who have served as tutors and tutees.

What about liability issues with having a peer be responsible for providing support to a student with a disability?

We have not had any issues with liability in the thirty years that we have been using peer tutors. Students are paired carefully and are always under the supervision of adults. If a student requires significant physical, medical, or behavioral support, then a paraprofessional is assigned to that student to provide that support in addition to the peer tutor. A peer tutor is never put in a position that would require them to be liable for the student, replace an educator, or assume the role of a paraprofessional.

Meet Kira and Isabel

Kira Sedore, who appears in figure 2.1, served as a peer tutor for over three years in high school. As a freshman, she was introduced to a classmate named Isabel, who a peer tutor was supporting in the same "surviving high school" general education class that she was attending. After spending time with Isabel, Kira realized that she wanted to not only be her friend but also help her in other classes. It was then that Kira enrolled in the peer tutoring course, and she continued to do so for each remaining year of her high school career.

Source: © 2026 by Elizabeth Castagnera. Used with permission.

Figure 2.1: *Kira (left) and Isabel (right).*

Kira states:

> Peer tutoring really broadened my horizons and expanded how I think about the world. Before high school, I had never met anyone with a disability, and so the peer tutoring course ended up teaching me a lot about friendship, empathy for others, and thinking outside the box to solve problems. It also made me realize that I wanted to teach, which is something I would not have pictured

> myself doing before peer tutoring! (K. Sedore, personal communication, June 4, 2025)

Kira is currently working as a paraprofessional for students with extensive support needs, and she loves her job. She is majoring in sociology at San Diego State University and plans to become a special education teacher once she is done with school. As a future educator, Kira believes that her experience as a peer tutor will absolutely benefit her. She says:

> The peer tutoring course laid the foundation for me of what is important in special education. The lessons I was taught about friendship, communication, and disability in general will stick with me for life and definitely influence how I work now and how I will work as an educator. (K. Sedore, personal communication, June 4, 2025)

Kira says this about her time:

> My most memorable time as a peer tutor was graduating with the students that I peer tutored. There were several students in the same graduating class as me and being able to graduate with them after being their peer tutor and friend for years was such an amazing experience. (K. Sedore, personal communication, June 4, 2025)

Meet Paola and Angel

Paola Castro, who appears in figure 2.2, served as a peer tutor during her senior year of high school. She enrolled in the course because she was short on credits for graduation, not realizing the impact the peer tutoring course would have on her. Even though she was a peer tutor for only one school year, it ended up being one of the most meaningful and rewarding experiences she had in high school:

Source: © 2026 by Elizabeth Castagnera. Used with permission.

Figure 2.2: *Paola (left) with Angel (right).*

> It wasn't just about helping others academically, it was about building personal relationships with the students, learning patience, and realizing how much I enjoy being there for people. That class quickly became the favorite part of my school day. It reminded me that even during hard times, I was still doing something good and meaningful, and that always made me feel better. (P. Castro, personal communication, June 5, 2025)

Paola plans to be a registered nurse. She currently attends Southwestern College in California and is highly focused on finishing her prerequisites so she can apply to the nursing program. Paola also likes to bake and has a small strawberries and cream business in Rosarito, Mexico. She believes that her experiences as a peer tutor will benefit her in the medical field:

> As a peer tutor, I learned how important patience, empathy, and clear communication are. I had to learn how to support someone based on their individual needs, and that's something that will also be super important when caring for patients. Being a peer tutor helped me grow not just as a student, but as a future healthcare provider. It reminded me how meaningful it is to help others and to make people feel seen and cared for. (P. Castro, personal communication, June 5, 2025)

Paola says this about her experience:

> The times I remember most during my senior year were the Fridays I spent with Angel, the peer student I worked with. Every Friday, I'd bring us lunch from one of his favorite fast-food restaurants and we would eat together. Those moments were special to me because we connected over something simple that we both enjoyed (good food). He would always let me know with his facial expressions how much he liked what I brought, and I could tell he really appreciated it. Sharing those lunches helped us build a stronger relationship, and it made our time together feel more meaningful. (P. Castro, personal communication, June 5, 2025)

Meet Megan and Rachel

Megan Tomlin, who appears in figure 2.3, was a peer tutor all four years of her high school career. She initially enrolled in the course because she needed an elective class, and when she saw peer tutoring as an option, she wanted to help! In addition to being a peer tutor during the school day, Megan volunteered her time to support students so they could be involved in extracurricular activities. During her junior year, she approached

Source: © *2026 by Rebecca Brooks. Used with permission.*

Figure 2.3: *Rachel (left) with Megan (right).*

administration and the special education staff with her strong conviction that Rachel (on the left in figure 2.3) not be singled out at graduation by having an adult aide walking next to her during the graduation ceremony. Megan requested that she be able to support Rachel. She also asked for permission to wear a cap and gown herself to blend in with other students as she supported Rachel during the ceremony. Graduation was a success. It has been over twenty years since they walked through graduation, and the two have remained great friends.

Megan says this about her time as a tutor:

> Being a peer tutor is what led me to choose the career I am in today! I am a special education teacher and plan to return to school to receive a master's degree in special education. I have many memorable moments as a peer tutor, but my favorite is all of the lifelong friendships I have made by being a peer tutor! (M. Tomlin, personal communication, August 4, 2025)

Meet Katie and Andrea

Katie Ellison and Andrea Norton, who appear in figure 2.4, are cousins. Katie received peer tutor support in high school, and Andrea was a peer tutor. Katie loved attending her high school with her friends. She was on the swim team and actively participated in campuswide events. She was that friend you could go to for anything and always had a smile on her face! Teachers were always excited to find out she was enrolled in their classes, as she was known as a student who lit up a room. Katie graduated high school and continues to pursue her passion for swimming by remaining active in swim meets. She also loves dancing and theater, often displaying her talent in local productions.

Source: © 2026 by Rebecca Brooks. Used with permission.

Figure 2.4: *Katie (left) and Andrea (right).*

Andrea knew she wanted to be a special education teacher and to have real-life experience working with students with special needs. She also wanted to see what inclusion in action looked like, so she enrolled in a yearlong peer tutoring course, where she supported a student named Chris in an English language arts class. She feels her experience as a peer tutor benefited her not only as a person but also as a future educational professional. Andrea went on to become a middle school special education teacher for ten years, where she educated students with mild to moderate support needs. She is currently an independent facilitator working with Southern California regional centers, where she advocates for clients and their families to receive services and assists them with the self-determination program. Additionally, she runs a nonprofit organization that provides services for adults with developmental disabilities that works to enable, empower, and enlighten individuals in a positive and engaging environment.

Katie had this to say about having a peer tutor:

> I really liked all my peer tutors! I enjoyed my time with all of them. They helped in my classes. They read things aloud to me and help me with my own reading. Because of them, I understood things in the class and became a better reader. I think everyone should have a peer tutor! (K. Ellison, personal communication, July 27, 2025)

Andrea had this to say about her experience as a tutor:

> For weekly vocabulary quizzes, I would help Chris study beforehand. As we talked about the meaning of each word, we would make up a hand movement that described its meaning. During the test, he would remember and associate the hand movements with the words. With this, Chris and I had a blast waving our hands around, gaining many stares from passersby in the hallways and he was truly learning new words at the same time. [With the year coming to an end], my days will not be the same without him. I wonder if I have had the same effect on him that he has had on me. I hope I have. (A. Norton, personal communication, June 1, 2007)

Meet Sarah and Julia

Sarah Simpson, who appears with Julia Bendas in figure 2.5, was placed in the peer tutoring course due to a conflict in her schedule. She had never heard of the peer tutoring course before and was not familiar with the roles and responsibilities of peer tutors. She arrived to class on her first day a little apprehensive and unsure of what to expect. She was paired with Julia because Julia was enrolled in a science class Sarah took the previous school year, so she knew the content and class structure. Julia benefited so much from having a peer tutor who understood the labs!

Source: © 2026 by Rebecca Brooks. Used with permission.

Figure 2.5: Sarah (left) and Julia (right).

As Sarah navigated her role as a peer tutor, receiving support from the special and general educators, she became more and more comfortable and confident in her new role. By the third week, she was set on remaining in the class, and she shared that she was not only enjoying it but already reaping the benefits. Sarah was incredibly grateful for her experience, stating that it forever changed her.

Sarah had this to say about her time as a peer tutor:

> I will be honest when I say that before being a peer tutor, I thought that students with disabilities could not perform in school in the same way as other students. However, Julia opened my eyes to a completely different perspective on the world. I got to know Julia and began to see how smart she really was! Julia and I developed a strong bond, not just as peer tutor and student, but as friends. I can only hope that others can experience the joy of peer tutoring. (S. Simpson, personal communication, June 9, 2008)

Julia received peer tutor support when attending her classes. She always looked forward to her classes. Being able to have peer tutor support always seemed like a bonus to Julia, as she loved meeting new people and connecting with others. She also enjoyed attending football games and school dances. Her caring personality lent itself to her passion for helping others. After graduating high school, she went to work at a preschool to teach young children with disabilities. She is currently a classroom aide in a second-grade general education classroom.

Julia had this to say about having a peer tutor:

> I felt really good about having peer tutors support me. They were very smart and kind. I liked getting to know them. They helped me with homework and walking around the school. Sometimes, it was just a matter of being with me, talking with me, and sitting with me in my classes. (J. Bendas, personal communication, May 22, 2025)

WHAT PEER TUTORS DO

Peer tutors can provide a wide range of support, including prompting, clarification of classroom directions, implementation of teacher-directed accommodations and modifications, and any other assistance the student needs. Peer tutors can provide support to students in any general education class—core academic courses as well as electives.

The roles of a peer tutor are fluid because some students only need assistance getting to and from their classrooms, while others require one-to-one support for the entire class period. In addition, some students may require support for the entire class at the beginning of the school year but, after some time, can increasingly become more independent and require less peer support. While peer tutors are most often paired with students who have extensive support needs, such as students with intellectual and developmental disabilities, you can also assign them to assist students with mild to moderate support needs, such as those with specific learning disabilities.

Ideally, students are enrolled in general education classes for the entire school day. Therefore, the special educator will have time to support the everyday logistics of a peer tutoring course. However, if all students with disabilities are not enrolled in general education classes 100 percent of their day, students can be scheduled to be in general education classes during the same periods. This means that during those periods of the school day, the special educators are available to both support the peer tutoring program and co-teach in the general education classrooms. For example, if the school has six periods and if all students are included in general education four periods of the school day, attempt to schedule students in a wide variety of general education classes in periods 2 through 5. Doing so ensures that during those four periods, the special educator is available where they are needed most, such as supporting peer tutors or students or co-teaching in general education classrooms.

Research shows that peer tutors provide academic and social support in many ways. For example, peer-mediated interventions for students with autism—one-to-one peer tutor support in a general education high school classroom, for example—are not only feasible but effective both socially and academically, and can address IEP goals (Carter et al., 2019). At the end of the day, the support a peer tutor provides is driven by the student's IEP and is based on what can best help them access curricula and activities and participate in all learning. This includes both academic and social learning.

The types of support that a peer tutor might provide to a student include the following.

- Assisting the student with locating their classrooms
- Assisting the student with assignments
- Helping the student stay on task
- Reminding the student to write down homework assignments and assisting them as needed
- Reminding the student to complete and turn in homework and assisting them as needed

- Reading materials aloud to the student
- Assisting the student with note taking
- Reviewing class content with the student
- Reading the in-class assigned materials to the student to ensure they understand the task
- Breaking down instructions into smaller chunks and clarifying as needed
- Reiterating and explaining instructions
- Summarizing information for the student
- Studying for assessments with the student
- Assisting the student with maintaining and organizing their belongings
- Assisting the student with projects or presentations
- Facilitating the student's participation in cooperative group learning activities
- Providing simple teacher-directed accommodations and modifications
- Providing levels of prompting
- Facilitating social interactions
- Advocating for the student and supporting them in advocating for themselves
- Modeling appropriate and effective social skills
- Assisting educators in creating adapted materials
- Serving as an additional communication link between general and special educators
- Sharing their expertise in particular subjects

Can peer tutors be included as support in the IEP?

Yes. If an IEP team in the United States determines support is needed for the student's *free appropriate public education*, peer tutor support can be added. Some school districts have a section on the IEP's accommodations and modifications page where *peer tutor support* can be checked. If a school district does not have such a section, the IEP team can add it as a support or as an addendum to the IEP. If peer tutor support is written into the IEP, it is important to discuss the plan for when a peer tutor is absent. That might include a substitute peer tutor, natural peer support in the class, or a paraprofessional, for example.

Do peer tutors decide which accommodations and modifications to provide to students?

Peer tutors cannot make decisions about what accommodations and modifications to provide. However, they can be tasked, by a licensed educator, to provide accommodations and modifications. For example, an educator can ask a peer tutor to highlight specific vocabulary words on a study guide or draw lines on an activity sheet for a student to write answers on. While peer tutors may come up with very creative ideas to adapt an assignment or activity, instruct them to seek an educator's guidance and approval before implementing.

Can a peer tutor provide support by joining their tutee on a field trip?

Absolutely! All educators would just need to communicate to ensure logistics are agreed on, permission slips are signed, and a structured support plan is in place.

SUMMARY

Peer tutors are students who want to help others succeed. While they may enter the classroom with a wide range of experiences and skills, all students are capable of becoming effective peer supports for others. Peer tutors can provide a wide array of assistance, which allows them to contribute their individual strengths. Due to this, peer tutoring enables all students, regardless of academic level, to participate as meaningful tutors and positively impact their peers. Peer tutors are just as essential in helping students with academic skills as they are in helping them in elective courses, such as music, art, and physical education.

Chapter 3 shifts focus to the practical side, offering educators step-by-step guidance on how to implement a peer tutoring course at the high school level.

PEER TUTOR TRAINING SESSIONS AT A GLANCE

An educator can use this reproducible as a snapshot or checklist of what to cover in all the training sessions, as well as a space for writing reflections about each session. Materials needed for each session are also listed.

Session One: Inclusive Education, Peer Tutor Expectations, and Digital Portfolio Project

The included activities follow. You can check them off as you complete them.

- ☐ Life-is-sweeter-with-chocolate activity (icebreaker)
- ☐ Introduction to inclusive education
- ☐ Benefits of inclusive education (Venn diagram)
- ☐ Responsibilities and expectations of peer tutors
- ☐ Respectful language
- ☐ Dot-and-circle activity
- ☐ Peer tutor digital portfolio project
- ☐ Homework

The required materials follow. You can check them off as you procure them.

- ☐ Boxes of assorted cream chocolates
- ☐ "Benefits of Inclusive Education" handout (page 95)
- ☐ "Tips for Being a Successful Peer Tutor" handout (page 96)
- ☐ "Respect" handout (page 97)
- ☐ "Person-First and Identity-First Language" handout (page 98)
- ☐ "Digital Portfolio Project" handout (page 99)
- ☐ "Digital Portfolio Project Rubric" handout (page 102)

Here, record what worked about the session, what didn't, and why.

Session Two: Support Strategies and Curriculum Accessibility

The included activities follow.

- ☐ Levels of prompting
- ☐ Curriculum accessibility
- ☐ Homework

The required materials follow.

- ☐ "Teaching Strategies and Accommodations" handout (page 111)
- ☐ "Student Case Studies for Curriculum Accessibility" handout (page 114)
- ☐ "Levels of Prompting" handout (page 116)
- ☐ General education assignment

Here, record what worked about the session, what didn't, and why.

Session Three: Communication

The included activities follow.

- ☐ Definitions of *communication*, *language*, and *speech*
- ☐ Receptive versus expressive language with What am I trying to say? activity
- ☐ Insights from a speech-language pathologist
- ☐ Homework

The required materials follow.

- ☐ Communication cards

  Create your own using index cards; see the What am I trying to say? activity in the Receptive Versus Expressive Language section (page 119). Make each A-B pair on the same color index card. For example, put the A *I'm hungry* card and the B *I'm hungry* card on yellow index cards, the A *I'm sad* card and the B *I'm sad* card on blue index cards, and so on.

Here, record what worked about the session, what didn't, and why.

Session Four: Social Inclusion

The included activities follow.

- ☐ Friendship quote interpretation
- ☐ Friendship qualities and circle of friends

- ☐ Facilitation of social interactions
- ☐ Facilitation of student involvement in group activities
- ☐ Friendship videos
- ☐ Homework

The required materials follow.

- ☐ "Circle of Friends" handout (page 132)
- ☐ "Perception Scripts" handout (page 133)
- ☐ "Strategies for Facilitating Social Interactions—Example Student Amari" handout (page 134)
- ☐ "Strategies for Facilitating Social Interactions" handout (page 135)
- ☐ "Scenarios for Student Involvement" handout (page 136)
- ☐ A video of your choice

Here, record what worked about the session, what didn't, and why.

Session Five: Book Talk

The included activities follow.

- ☐ Book talk
- ☐ Homework

The required materials follow.

- ☐ Access to a class set of a book (teacher's choice)
- ☐ Discussion questions, such as the "*Stuck in Neutral* by Terry Trueman" or "*Out of My Mind* by Sharon M. Draper" handout (pages 142 and 145)

Here, record what worked about the session, what didn't, and why.

Session Six: Research Project

The included activity follows.

- ☐ Research project
- ☐ Homework

The required materials follow.

- ☐ Student access to computers or Chromebooks
- ☐ School library (if possible)
- ☐ "Research Project" handout (page 153)
- ☐ "Research Project Rubric" handout (page 154)

Here, record what worked about the session, what didn't, and why.

Session Seven: Digital Portfolio Presentations

The included activity follows.

- ☐ Presentations

The required materials follow.

- ☐ Projector and screen for student presentations

Here, record what worked about the session, what didn't, and why.

CHAPTER 3

Peer Tutoring Course Logistics

While there are many benefits to offering a peer tutoring course at the high school level, the logistics can appear daunting. The course components are often similar across different school sites, but the process may differ depending on each school's structure. First and foremost, it is important for the school to have administrative support for the new course. Special educators need to work collaboratively with their administrators so everyone has a clear understanding of (a) the critical role peer tutors serve in providing an equitable education for students with disabilities, (b) the benefits everyone receives, and (c) the course details, once prepared. Share peer tutoring benefits—for students with disabilities as well as the peer tutors themselves. In addition, explore the positive impact peer tutoring has on the school's entire culture.

Next, a team of educators develops a sound course curriculum and syllabus for the peer tutoring course. It is ideal to have both general and special educators collaborate, bringing their expertise and perspective to the instructional planning and decision-making processes. If possible, the educator who plans to serve as the teacher of record for the peer tutoring course should be part of this process.

It is important for the course to be created in a way that meets the needs of peer tutors and the students with disabilities they will support. Once the course curriculum and syllabus are approved, the next steps are getting the course included in the elective section of the school's course catalog and advertising the course. At this point, it is essential that stakeholders—including administrators, faculty, parents, and students—have a thorough understanding of the description and requirements of the peer tutoring course.

The final step is implementing the course. A functional organization system is key when pairing peer tutors with students with disabilities across numerous general education classes. An organization system needs to include a structure for overseeing peer tutors, taking attendance, maintaining daily communication, and providing training and ongoing support.

A list of these steps follows, with the rest of the chapter providing the necessary details for executing each step.

1. Gain administrative support.
    - Relay the importance of peer tutoring.
    - Lay out the research-backed benefits for everyone.
    - Provide course details (which may be required in full after you work with your team).
2. Develop the course.
    - Confirm the teacher of record.
    - Determine prerequisites (if any).
    - Detail the course curriculum.
    - Decide on grading guidelines.
3. Advertise the course.
    - Educate faculty and staff (especially counselors).
    - Advertise to students and families.
4. Implement the course.
    - Determine tutee and peer tutor pairings.
    - Decide on a communication system.
    - Implement an attendance system.
    - Create an organization system (one that works for the teacher of record).

ADMINISTRATIVE SUPPORT

Most schools must present new courses to the school board for approval and follow its guidelines in adding a new course. Be prepared for this process to take some time. Later in this chapter (page 55), we offer some interim solutions so peer support can be put in place during the time the course is being developed and awaiting approval.

When educators have decided peer support is a necessity at their school, they pose to their principal the idea for a peer tutoring course. They provide research and anecdotes about the importance and benefits of peer tutoring while making it clear that not only students who receive special education services experience positive effects. If the principal approves, the educators construct the course and present its details for final approval. While part 2 of this book provides a ready-to-use peer tutoring course curriculum, it should be customized to meet the specific needs of student populations and individual school sites. For example, a school may have a specific learning management system or technology software applications that are used widely throughout the school. You can easily add discussions of accessibility concerning this technology, as well as specific support strategies, to session two (support strategies and curriculum accessibility).

First Meeting

The first step is to initiate a conversation with the administrative team at the school site and to help them understand the importance of peer tutoring and the need for a strong level of support for its implementation. If the concept of peer tutoring is new to the school, be prepared to share the following in detail.

- Explain the numerous short- and long-term benefits for students with disabilities, peer tutors, and educators. Refer to research that supports these claims, such as the sources we mentioned in chapter 1. Connect current research with the school's population and structure and students' needs.
- Describe how peer tutoring allows for educating all students in the least restrictive environment as outlined in IDEA (2004).
- Explain how implementing a peer tutoring elective course can deeply and positively impact a school's culture.
- Identify which educators are willing to develop and implement the program, along with the specific roles each is committing to.
- Share the ideal number of peer tutors you seek, taking into consideration the number of students who could benefit from a peer tutor and the number of general education classes they are enrolled in. For example, if twenty students with disabilities need peer tutor support, and all those students are enrolled in general education classes for six periods a day, then a minimum of 120 peer tutors would be needed. However, it is ideal to allow additional peer tutors to enroll, which helps ensure adequate support when peer tutors are absent.

It is imperative that administrators understand that peer tutoring is a benefit to not only students with disabilities but the entire school community. The impacts of peer tutoring spread across the entire school, and they even reach the surrounding community as students graduate and take with them everything they have learned from their peer tutoring experience.

Overall, be prepared to present the idea with enthusiasm—and to back it up with solid research—to an audience that may or may not be familiar with the educational practice of peer supports. Approach the meeting ready to explain both the basics of the peer tutoring concept, as well as the specific logistics of ensuring students with disabilities are provided peer support daily in general education classrooms. It is important for the administrative team to truly understand what you are proposing and how critical access to peer support is for students with disabilities to succeed in general education classrooms.

If administration is not amenable to adding a new course, be prepared to offer other solutions, such as those outlined in the Alternatives to a Peer Tutoring Course section (page 55). Be open to thinking creatively about alternatives unique to your school. Remember, it isn't about one specific course with a prescribed curriculum. Rather, it is about collaborating with your administration to determine what will work best at your school to provide students with the personal supports they need to access an equitable education and to succeed.

Subsequent Meetings

If your administrator gives the go-ahead on course creation and implementation, you will likely collaborate with administrators and counseling advisers to determine the steps necessary to have the course approved. Your peer tutoring course creation team will have to consider the following four aspects.

1. **How many credit hours to offer for completing the course:** It is useful to provide full elective credit for the course—rather than the half credit students are sometimes given—for two reasons. One, the work ethic and commitment required of peer tutors deserve a full-credit course. Two, a full-credit course keeps enrollment high, since students often seek additional course credits for graduation.
2. **Whether there will be prerequisites:** Possible prerequisites include a minimum grade point average or grade level, letters of recommendation, and prior experience with leadership or tutoring. While the goal of prerequisites is to ensure well-qualified peer tutors, know that they can potentially exclude students who would be fantastic peer tutors, which is a loss for everyone. The best prerequisites are wanting to help others and being open to learning support strategies. To learn more about these considerations, read the Prerequisites section (page 45).
3. **Whether students can repeat the course:** Many students enjoy the course to such an extent that they request to enroll in it more than once during

their high school career. This is beneficial because as the peer tutors become more experienced, they provide even better support. Educators are able to capitalize on peer tutors' skills as they become more experienced. However, in some instances, students are not allowed to take courses more than once for credit. In that case, it may be practical to design the course proposal to resemble other out-of-classroom experiences—for example, with teaching assistants and office workers—that students can typically do more than once. Another possible solution is to create several course proposals at once, such as Peer Tutoring 1, Peer Tutoring 2, and so on.

4. **How many students can enroll in the course per course period:** It is ideal to accept enough peer tutors to be paired with the number of students who could benefit from peer tutor support each period or block of the school day. Importantly, consider whether to accept more peer tutors than tutees in order to have extra peer tutors to serve as substitute tutors when someone is absent or a student drops the course. Extra peer tutors can also work with educators to make simple curricular accommodations and modifications. For example, an educator who is creating a visual study guide for a student could task a peer tutor with finding the correct photos online. They could also ask peer tutors to highlight key terms or instructions on activity sheets, for example, or to assist with adding adhesive to laminated pictures for a visual schedule.

As a group, administrators and educators can work together to ensure the peer tutoring course creation team takes the proper steps to develop a peer tutoring course. Here are ways that administrators can support educators through this process.

- Provide guidance to educators on the new course approval process for the school or district.
- Share with the peer tutoring course team any experience with—or knowledge of—peer tutoring programs. If none, share any support that can be provided moving forward.
- Seek knowledge from other administrators who have had success with peer tutoring courses at their school sites.
- Use the expertise of administrators experienced with peer tutoring programs to add suggestions of the most effective way to implement a peer tutoring course on the campus.
- Communicate with all school staff, promoting this new learning opportunity for students on the campus.

- Ensure that all educators and staff are committed to maintaining confidentiality when working with peer tutors (regarding the Family Educational Rights and Privacy Act [FERPA, 1974] and other federal, state, and provincial laws). This includes training all staff not to share personal information with peer tutors about, for example, disability diagnoses or any aspects of IEPs. Create a routine of only holding discussions about students in areas away from peer tutors and designate safe locations for all personal documents to maintain privacy.

How difficult is the process to achieve peer tutoring course approval?

The process can take some time. Collaborate with administrators to learn the process your school site uses. Find out if any other schools in your district have a peer tutoring course, or one that is similar, that you could implement at your school site. Seek support and guidance from colleagues who have developed new courses. In the meantime, while developing the course, consider the alternative ways to provide peer tutor support that we discuss later in this chapter (page 55).

COURSE DEVELOPMENT

The next step is to develop the course structure and curriculum. Meet with fellow teachers who will be involved in developing the course, and collectively create your school's peer tutoring course. Remember that general educators can be of particular value in this process, as they will be the ones hosting peer tutors in their classes.

Ideally, the peer tutoring course creation team should consist of the following individuals.

- The educator who will oversee the students (also known as *teacher of record*)
- The special educators who will oversee the students with disabilities requiring peer tutoring support
- The general educators who will have the tutored students in their classrooms receiving the peer tutor support

Equally important is to consider including any paraprofessionals or related service providers who have meaningful insights to contribute. Determine what the prerequisites will be (if any), what the curriculum content will be, when the course will be offered, and how the course will be graded. Once you decide on this information as a team, you can create a syllabus.

It is also important to consider the data that will need to be collected to support ongoing evaluation of the course. This data should both demonstrate the program's effectiveness and provide meaningful feedback to guide any necessary improvements after implementation.

- The number of students with extensive support needs who enrolled and successfully participated in general education courses as a result of the peer tutoring course
- The meaningful content and data collected in the digital portfolio project
- Educator feedback
- Peer tutor evaluation forms
- Peer tutor self-evaluation forms

Teacher of Record

Before considering the options, know that more than one educator can serve as a teacher of record for peer tutoring. A number of educators could teach sections of a peer tutoring course at one school site. While any teacher can oversee the peer tutoring course, special educators are selected most often. Table 3.1 (page 46) offers considerations when choosing whether to have a general education or special education teacher be the teacher of record.

An educator who manages students as teacher of record has the students on their attendance roster, issues grades for the course, and is responsible for daily student supervision. The Course Advertisement section (page 51) of this chapter addresses the importance of recruiting students to serve as substitutes.

For the purpose of the remainder of this book, the special educator serves as the teacher of record in the examples we provide.

Prerequisites

When considering prerequisites, know that while you can require them for the course, academic ability and previously passed courses are not always necessary and can exclude students who could be amazing peer tutors. A review of the literature can help educators feel comfortable eliminating prerequisites that would preclude some students from becoming a peer tutor. By limiting (or not instituting) prerequisites, educators can provide a broader range of students the opportunity

Table 3.1: *Teacher of Record Considerations*

General Education Teacher	Special Education Teacher
Benefits: • Having the peer tutor listed on their attendance roster allows the tutor to check in directly with that teacher at the start of class (instead of arriving late). • Some general educators may take on more responsibility overseeing and instructing the peer tutors' day-to-day roles if those students were on their roster. **Drawbacks:** • The peer tutor must explicitly seek out the special educator to communicate the tutee's needs.	**Benefits:** • Frequent contact with tutors who support the students with disabilities on their caseload allows for daily communication of the students' individual needs. If the special educators provide input for any accommodations and modifications for the general education classes, they will find it beneficial to interact daily with the peer tutors who attend those classes. • When students with disabilities are included in general education classes for the majority (or entirety) of the school day, special educators may have time at the beginning and end of each period to oversee the peer tutors. If needed and available, paraprofessionals can help conduct an organized check-in and checkout. • These special educators are aware of absences, so they can send a substitute peer tutor or make other support arrangements. **Drawbacks:** • The peer tutor often arrives slightly late to general education classrooms (because of check-in).

to participate (Travers & Carter, 2022b). Hilary E. Travers and Erik W. Carter's (2022b) literature review shows that a wide variety of students without disabilities have the potential to contribute meaningfully to peer-mediated interventions.

All students have strengths. Those strengths can be homed in and used to provide support to students in a wide variety of areas. For example, a peer tutor may not be strong in the areas of reading and writing, but they may have excellent skills in other areas, such as mathematics. You could assign that student to support another student in geometry. Similarly, a student may struggle academically themselves but may be an incredible artist or athlete, so they could be a peer tutor in an art class or physical education class.

Students with disabilities can serve as peer tutors. For example, a student with a mild to moderate learning disability who has below-grade-level mathematics skills can be a peer tutor for a student with an intellectual disability who is learning to identify numbers and tell time. Often, students with learning disabilities—or those who are learning English—make excellent peer tutors for students who are beginning to learn to read and write. They experience great pride in realizing that they can teach someone else to read, write, or complete work with the use of pictures or communication devices in a high school classroom. In addition, as we mentioned in the Benefits of Peer Tutoring section (page 16), it's possible that peer tutors will improve their own reading and writing by teaching another student these skills. A research review (Wang, Bettini, & Cheyney, 2013) finds that students with disabilities can be productive, responsible peer tutors. Students with learning disabilities and emotional and behavioral disorders report that serving as a peer tutor is actually more impactful than being tutored—a finding that highlights how peer tutoring programs enhance the academic achievements, behavior, and social outcomes of all students (Watts, Bryant, & Carroll, 2019).

Students in all kinds of unique circumstances can still be an incredible support to other students. For example, a student who had a disciplinary record for inappropriate language enrolled as a peer tutor in one of our classes. We discussed the importance of appropriate language and the role model he would become for others. He shared that using inappropriate language was a habit and a result of his surroundings outside of school. When he realized that others would look to him as an example and that the student he was going to support might imitate what he said, he sat up a little straighter and said he wanted to try. Not only was this student an excellent role model, but he took it on himself to teach the student appropriate trending slang so they could have their own teenage greetings. He later shared that being a peer tutor actually motivated him to improve his language, and he felt the experience benefited him as much as it did the student he supported.

Another student—who was dealing with emotional issues—felt out of place at school and disconnected. When she became a peer tutor, she was very willing to help but was quiet and reserved. She shared with her teachers that she was struggling socially due to emotional issues stemming from outside of school. It was evident that social interactions were hard for her, but she was kind and gentle with others. She wasn't extroverted and needed some extra prompting, and she still provided excellent peer tutor support. As the semester continued, she and the tutee developed a friendship. She later shared that being a peer tutor and having the new friendship gave her strength to get through the school day.

Some students have lots of absences. Yet that doesn't mean they shouldn't be allowed to be a peer tutor. One student was called to the office for a meeting with their parents and teachers. On arrival, everyone was notified that the student, who had a history of absences, had missed more than the maximum number of days allowed for a semester. However, the administrator had one question: Why was peer tutoring the only class they had perfect attendance in? The student explained what their academic struggles were and how the peer tutoring course was the only class where they felt competent. Examples like these reinforce the importance of keeping an open door to a peer tutoring elective course. Sometimes, the students who need it most aren't only the students with disabilities.

Some schools may choose to make grade levels a prerequisite, limiting the course to only upperclassmen. However, if a peer tutor's grade level is considered when assigning them to a particular class, then this limitation is not necessary. For example, a ninth-grade student would most likely not be assigned to support a student in a twelfth-grade core class. It truly should come down to strengths, not grade point averages or grade levels. This keeps the doors open to all students. Many times, the students who are least likely to be recommended for peer tutoring turn out to be the best peer tutors! They often discover strengths and interests they didn't even know they had when given the chance to support other students.

Never doubt that all students have something to contribute and can effectively teach or support other students. Schools with peer tutoring courses that require students to be at a certain grade level, demonstrate a minimum academic ability level, or maintain a certain grade point average will truly miss out on many students who could be extraordinary peer tutors. The following true story exemplifies this. Brittany was diagnosed with a learning disability and had an IEP. Reading was especially challenging for her as a junior. She decided to enroll in her high school's peer tutoring course and was paired with a student who was learning to read sight words—something Brittany could easily support the student to accomplish.

One day, Brittany's grandmother called the peer tutoring teacher to share how grateful she was for the course and how happy she was for her granddaughter. She explained that reading had always been difficult for Brittany, which had impacted her confidence and self-esteem about her own learning. She said that since Brittany had enrolled in the peer tutoring course, she had been coming home excited to share her peer tutoring experiences. Brittany told her grandmother that even though she had a hard time reading herself, she was realizing that she was able to teach someone else to read. With her voice cracking, Brittany's grandmother said that for the first time, she saw her granddaughter's self-esteem rise. Brittany knew she could help others and was beginning to believe in her own reading ability a little more. Success stories like this would not be possible if a prerequisite had been in place that excluded students with learning differences—like Brittany—from being a peer tutor.

Are some students just not capable of being a peer tutor?

Many students who would not likely be recommended for peer tutoring or who are struggling in their own classes find their niche in being a peer tutor. Some of the best peer tutors are those least expected to be. Be open to the idea of any student serving as a peer tutor. Truly get to know each student who is interested by asking the right questions. Strive to find each student's unique talents, interests, and strengths before turning them away. Just like a student in the classroom given the proper support and guidance, all students should have the opportunity to be peer tutors. It could be a transformational moment that could change a student's life.

Course Curriculum

Next, create and organize the peer tutoring course curriculum into a syllabus. The course curriculum consists of the instruction and activities provided throughout the course. It can be challenging to give this direct instruction, since peer tutors are out supporting students in general education classes instead of being all together for a class. Therefore, set aside time for training sessions for the peer tutors. A small number of trainings is all you need to ensure students understand their role and learn the support strategies.

The peer tutoring course curriculum in part 2 outlines seven training sessions. Most of these training sessions should occur as soon as possible once the school year begins in order to build tutors' capacity to support students in their assigned classes. One session per week is reasonable, given the amount of time it takes an educator to provide the trainings each period per day. This schedule also means that students with disabilities have to go to class unsupported one day of each of the seven weeks. In addition to the training sessions, you can give tutors a variety of assignments throughout the course to teach them the content of the sessions, such as inclusive education, communication, or social inclusion. Suggestions on how to schedule and implement the training sessions, along with lesson plans, are provided in part 2.

Grading

Because the peer tutoring course is taken for academic credit, it is essential for the course creation team to come to a consensus on how to grade peer tutors. Examples of peer tutoring course learning objectives follow.

- Comprehension of the principles of inclusive education
- Respect for student dignity
- Ability to describe disability using strength-based, person-first, or identity-first language
- Skills to provide one-to-one tutoring strategies
- Skills to communicate and collaborate effectively

Typically, peer tutoring grades are assessed based on the following five criteria.

1. **Attendance**
    - Daily attendance and punctuality
    - Communication of absences with the teacher of record
2. **Journal entries**
    - Daily entry
3. **Regular communication**
    - Communication with special educator
    - Communication with general educator
4. **Quality of support**
    - Thought and care given to providing support
    - Initiative in giving support
    - Effective communication with tutee
    - Focus and engagement
5. **Assignments**
    - Completion of training session activities
    - Completion of a digital portfolio

It is important to note that while the course includes valuable curriculum and training, the primary focus is not on the content or the various assignments but rather the quality of support the peer tutor provides. Few assignments are given, as the peer tutor should spend most of their time focused on providing effective support each day. For this reason, the most heavily weighted areas of a peer tutor's grade are their responsibilities as a peer tutor, which include attendance, communication, and the quality of the support they give.

One might measure the quality of support by the following.

- The thought and care the peer tutor dedicates to providing support and their initiative in providing support, such as by:

    - Demonstrating that they have thought about the best ways to support a student
    - Proposing creative ideas to ensure accessibility
    - Being mindful of their responsibilities as a peer tutor
    - Taking considerate actions that demonstrate respect
- The effectiveness of their communication with their tutee
- Being on task and engaged

Educators can assess the support a peer tutor gives through their interactions with the peer tutor and their observations of how the peer tutor relates with—and gives support to—the tutee.

While the teacher of record is the person who submits grades, it can be more comprehensive for both the special and general educator to have input on the grade. The "Peer Tutor Evaluation Form" (page 70) is a way to employ collaborative grading. The special educator and general educator complete the form separately to ensure inter-rater reliability, as each of these educators observes the student at different times. You can share this form with the peer tutor if you think it is necessary. The teacher of record can obtain information from the general educators via the emails and conversations that occur throughout the semester. To provide peer tutors with a way to monitor their own progress, you can ask them to complete the "Self-Evaluation Form" (page 72). Educators and peer tutors can complete these evaluations during grading periods to offer insight into tutors' overall effectiveness and quality. (Visit **go.SolutionTree.com/specialneeds** to download free reproducible versions of these evaluation forms.)

Course Advertisement

Advertising the course is always an important component to peer tutor enrollment. Advertising ensures two things: a correct understanding of (1) what the course's purpose is and who can enroll and (2) a peer tutor's roles and responsibilities. It also can significantly increase enrollment. However, it is especially critical when the course is brand new and unfamiliar to faculty, staff, students, and families—areas we address in the following sections.

Educate Faculty and Staff

It is important to inform all faculty and staff about the peer tutoring course so they understand the roles of peer tutors on the school campus. By learning about the course, faculty members—especially counselors—can recommend it to students as a possible elective course for them to enroll in. Consult with the staff member responsible for creating the catalog so the correct description is included, providing them with a flyer for guidance.

It is also critical to ensure the course appears in the correct location of the catalog. If it is listed under a special education section, know that most students without disabilities will not see the course offering. Instead, include the description in the general elective section and, ideally, list it as a suggested course for any related career pathways the school offers (such as health sciences, education, human services, social services, and so on). Share the flyer with the faculty adviser and student officers of any related campus clubs, such as Future Teachers of America or HOSA–Future Health Professionals. Figure 3.1 provides an example course catalog description for peer tutoring.

HIGH SCHOOL PEER TUTORING COURSE:

This course develops skills to effectively support students with disabilities and deepens the understanding of diverse learning styles. Peer tutors will help students with disabilities understand classroom materials while fostering their participation in class activities and facilitating their interactions with other students. This course enhances knowledge in inclusive education, peer tutoring, and disability through seven structured training sessions. Guidance and support from classroom teachers, special education teachers, classroom aides, speech-language pathologists, occupational therapists, physical therapists, and mobility therapists are provided.

While this course is open to all students, it is highly recommended for students interested in pursuing careers in helping professions such as teaching; speech-language pathology; occupational, physical, or mobility therapy; counseling; psychology; healthcare; and social work.

Figure 3.1: *Example course catalog description for peer tutoring course.*

Advertise to Students and Families

You can advertise the course and provide its detailed description in a number of ways.

- **Post bright descriptive flyers around the school hallways:** Prior to creating the flyer, communicate with school administration and the special education department regarding specific school and district policies and procedures for advertising the course. You can see an example of what might work for your school in figure 3.2.

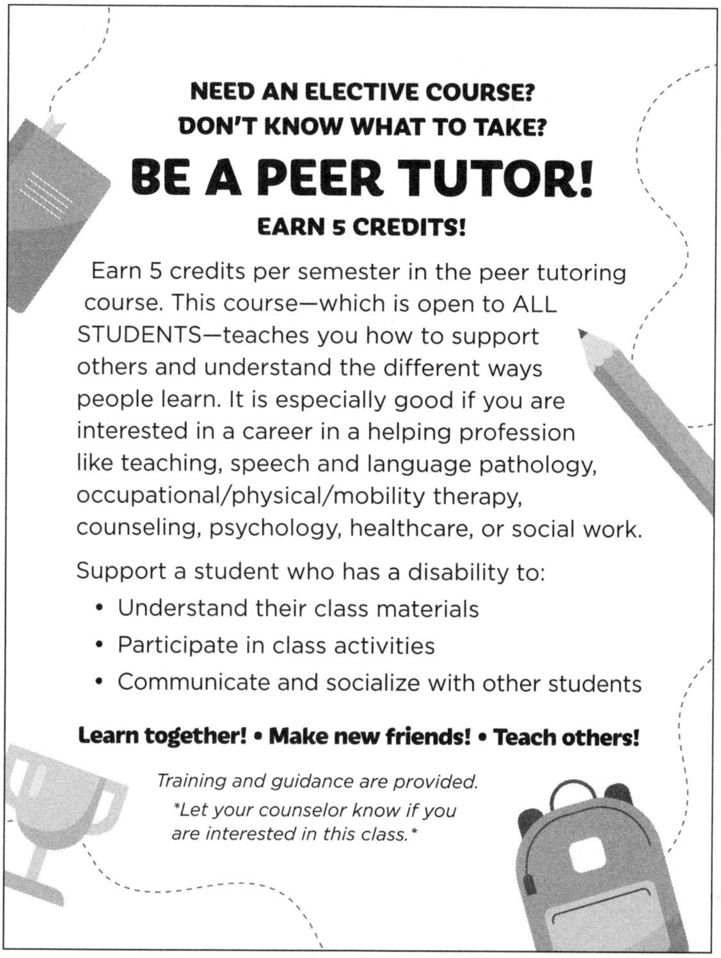

NEED AN ELECTIVE COURSE?
DON'T KNOW WHAT TO TAKE?

BE A PEER TUTOR!

EARN 5 CREDITS!

Earn 5 credits per semester in the peer tutoring course. This course—which is open to ALL STUDENTS—teaches you how to support others and understand the different ways people learn. It is especially good if you are interested in a career in a helping profession like teaching, speech and language pathology, occupational/physical/mobility therapy, counseling, psychology, healthcare, or social work.

Support a student who has a disability to:

- Understand their class materials
- Participate in class activities
- Communicate and socialize with other students

Learn together! • Make new friends! • Teach others!

Training and guidance are provided.
Let your counselor know if you are interested in this class.

Figure 3.2: *Sample flyer to advertise a peer tutoring course.*

- **Give flyers to counselors and ask them to share the information with students when they determine class schedules:** Counselors can recommend the course to students who have expressed an interest in a career helping others, as well as to those who need to choose an elective and aren't familiar with the course as an option. Counselors can also share the flyer when they meet incoming students and families from surrounding feeder schools.
- **Keep stacks of the flyer on the desks of academic advisers and in a visible location in the counseling office:** It is important for the flyer to be easily accessible to students who are visiting the counseling office to discuss their class schedule. In addition, provide all faculty and staff with a brightly colored flyer to post in their classrooms and share with students. You can also share the flyer digitally with faculty (who can

then post it on their learning management systems, as appropriate) and with the person charged with writing newsletters (who can include it in communications going home to families).

- **Ask teachers of core freshmen classes to dedicate five minutes in each period to explaining the course:** They would clarify three things—(1) what the elective is, (2) how students will see peer tutors in their classes throughout high school, and (3) how students can include their enrollment in the course on job, college, and scholarship applications.

Look for any and all opportunities to promote the peer tutoring course. For example, when the school hosts informational fairs (such as informational nights for incoming freshmen), tabling for the peer tutoring course is a great way to explain it to families. The educators who oversee the peer tutoring course can set up a booth and have current peer tutors (excepting possibly those courses in their inaugural year, of course, unless the school includes tutors from other schools) explain the course and answer questions from incoming students and families.

Wherever you're advertising, make sure that prospective students understand the course description. Address common misunderstandings by making the following clear.

- It is not a course for students to take if they want or need to be tutored themselves.
- Peer tutors do not need to be at the top of their class in a certain subject area to qualify for tutoring someone else.

Because of these common misperceptions, it is important to find ways to share knowledge of the course description and student eligibility.

If peer tutor enrollment is low, not all students will have the peer tutor support they require to be successful. If this is the case, while it is not ideal, peer tutors can be shared within a class or across classes.

Can a peer tutor receive credit for the general education class they are providing support in?

No. Peer tutors receive elective credit for the course they are enrolled in, which is peer tutoring. They do not receive credit for the class that they attend with the student they support, and they are not required to complete any of the course requirements for that general education class.

Alternatives to a Peer Tutoring Course

While an effective, organized peer tutoring course is not created overnight and will take some time to get approved, many students will still need peer tutor support as soon as possible. There are many options for implementing peer support in the interim. For example, schools often have the option for special or general educators to have students who are teacher assistants in their classrooms. If this is the case, either educator can have their teacher assistants take on the role of a peer tutor for a student with a disability. This is a great way to start peer tutoring prior to course approval and implementation.

Another option during this waiting period is to have students volunteer as peer tutors to complete community service hours. Since upperclassmen are typically enrolled in fewer classes during the school day, they often have extra time in their day to volunteer as a peer tutor. In addition, some high schools and honors programs require community service hours for graduation. For example, community service hours are a common part of a school's Portrait of a Graduate requirements that outline student success. Another idea is to include college students who are interested in volunteering or earning community service hours.

And last, natural peer support is always an option, with or without a structured peer tutoring system in place. As a reminder, *natural supports* are students who are already enrolled in the same general education class as the student needing support and are willing to give a helping hand. Teaching all students the skills to help others cannot be overstated, as "compassion cannot exist without empathy" (Riess, 2017, p. 77). Creating a class where all students are supported and feel as though they belong is the foundation for establishing an inclusive culture within a classroom.

Be creative in seeking out students who could serve as peer tutors! Often, many readily available individuals can serve as peer tutors. However, they may not be obvious until you really begin searching.

SYSTEMS FOR EFFECTIVE PEER TUTORING

After receiving your administrator's OK to offer the course, creating the content details with your course creation team, advertising the course through different avenues, and signing up students, it is time to implement the course itself. That means pairing tutors with students who have disabilities, as well as deciding on communication and attendance expectations and an organization system.

Table 3.2 (page 56) shares some of the typical barriers educators who have implemented such a course have experienced, as well as suggested actions to overcome those barriers.

Table 3.2: *Overcoming Barriers*

Barriers and Corresponding Actions
Barrier: There is a lack of buy-in from faculty, staff, students, or families due to peer tutoring being an unfamiliar resource. **Actions:** Provide professional learning or resources (such as a flyer) that cover key points regarding the specifics of the peer tutoring course and benefits for all students. Have the special educator discuss the course at IEP meetings.
Barrier: Not enough students are enrolling in the peer tutoring course. **Actions:** Collaborate with counselors and academic advisers to educate students on the course and recommend it! Increase course advertisement (for example, flyers in the counseling office, posters around the school, and announcements in the school broadcast, bulletin, or newspaper). Conduct short recruitment presentations in core classes to inform students of the course option. Set up booths at schoolwide events, such as orientations, freshmen preview nights, parent-teacher nights, and so on. See the Course Advertisement section (page 51) for more-detailed suggestions.
Barrier: The teacher of record lacks the time to oversee and support the peer tutors enrolled in the course. **Actions:** Block out time to fulfill the responsibilities of overseeing a peer tutoring course. If students with disabilities are included in general education classes *the entire school day*, the special educator should have the flexibility to arrange their day to support peer tutors. If students with disabilities are in general education classes for only *a portion of the school day*, consider enrolling these students in a variety of general education classes during the same periods of the day to allow the special educator to be available during those periods. Have paraprofessionals assist as needed so the special educator can be available to check in with peer tutors during the first five or ten minutes and the last five or ten minutes of each class period. Create an effective and efficient peer tutor communication system (such as journals and daily update forms).
Barrier: There isn't time to conduct peer tutor trainings. **Actions:** Obtain a substitute to cover the special educator's classroom for the day. This frees up the special educator so they can hold the training sessions. Invite qualified professionals to provide training (such as a speech-language pathologist for the communication training, a librarian for the research project training, and so on).
Barrier: We don't yet have an approved peer tutoring course. **Actions:** Explore the school site to determine creative ways to offer a peer tutoring option to students. For example, ask general education or special education teacher assistants to serve as peer tutors, or have students volunteer during a period they don't have a class in order to receive volunteer or community service hours. See the Alternatives to a Peer Tutoring Course section (page 55) for more-detailed suggestions.

The following sections look at potential student pairing, communication, attendance, and organization systems and provide considerations when implementing these systems.

Student Pairing System

Creating an effective way to pair students with peer tutors is essential. Careful pairing will make the experience more successful for both the peer tutor and the student receiving support. One way to successfully pair is to distribute the "Peer Tutor Survey" (page 74) on the first day of class. This survey collects the following pertinent information to aid in pairing tutors with tutees. Examples of imaginary students are included.

- **Grade level:** Grade level is sometimes a factor when pairing students, but not always. For example, a freshman could be very successful supporting a sophomore, junior, or senior in subjects like physical education, band, drama, or art—especially if they have strengths in those areas. However, as we mentioned earlier, a freshman peer tutor is not typically paired with a senior for a core academic class. Students should have the option of supporting a student in a class they have strengths in.
- **Current class schedule:** Be mindful of the classes peer tutors are currently enrolled in. Some general educators enjoy having a peer tutor who is also enrolled in their class during a different period or block. This can be an excellent opportunity for reinforcing content that the peer tutor is learning themselves. Educators often find that peer tutors who are familiar with the course structure and have exposure to the curriculum and instruction twice a day not only provide better support but learn more themselves. For example, imaginary student Daren was enrolled in an English language arts class with Mr. Barnett for his second-period class and would then return later in the school day as a peer tutor for a student in Mr. Barnett's fourth-period class. Daren was incredibly prepared to support a student in the class.
- **Interests and extracurricular activities:** Consider whether pairs share common interests or participate in similar extracurricular activities. When two people share common interests, it can strengthen their connection and increase mutual comfort levels. Pairs finding commonalities can also enhance their bond, sometimes leading to friendships.

- **Favorite classes:** If peer tutors previously took a particular class, enjoyed it, and were successful in it, they may be interested in being assigned to a student in that class. For example, Roxy had biology with Mr. Hurley during her sophomore year and is now an eleventh-grade peer tutor. She is a great support for a tenth-grade student this year in that same biology class with Mr. Hurley. Roxy already knows the curriculum, understands the assignments, and has had experience in the class with that teacher. This is an ideal pairing of a peer tutor and a student!
- **Personal experiences:** Some peer tutors have unique life or educational experiences that could contribute to considerations for pairings. For example, a peer tutor could have a family member who uses the same type of communication device as a current student. This knowledge could make the peer tutor's support more effective.

Some parents or guardians have requests regarding the tutor their child has. Sometimes, that means the family asks for a male or female specifically, a certain grade level, or a person they know personally. Try to honor those requests as much as possible. When it is not possible to honor specific requests, it is important to discuss with the family available options that will appropriately meet the student's needs. For example, a student could receive initial support from peers in the general education class while the special educator collaborates with the counselor and advertises across campus to identify a student who meets the criteria and is interested in joining the peer tutoring course. It is also important to determine any specific family requests *prior* to the start of the semester to allow for earlier and more effective planning.

Can a peer tutor provide support to a student outside the school day at an extracurricular activity?

Yes, a peer tutor can volunteer outside their assigned class time to provide peer tutor support at an extracurricular activity that is supervised by school faculty or staff. It can be a great opportunity to meet student needs when possible. We knew a student who was on the high school swim team and needed support during practice. Her English language arts peer mentor wanted to support her at after-school practices, so the special educator communicated with the swim coach and coordinated the times. In a different example, a student needed support watching the baseball games after school. (He was a huge baseball fan!) His peer tutor from the previous school year learned this about him. He and his former peer tutor developed a friendship and kept in touch. The former peer tutor offered to go with him to all the home games. A previous peer tutor experience turned into a wonderful natural support. This is above and beyond the peer tutoring course requirements, but the peer tutors wanted to volunteer.

In general, the "Peer Tutor Survey" (page 74) provides enough information to make the pairing process successful. However, sometimes you must change initial pairings. This can be due to a number of reasons.

- **Personality differences:** Students may communicate or interact in different ways. For example, some students are very outgoing, while others are more reserved; some prefer spontaneity, while others prefer structure. Although these differences can be complementary, in some cases, they may impact the pairing's effectiveness.
- **Learning style differences:** Students learn in different ways; they may differ in how they understand information, engage with content, and respond to instruction. For example, a tutor who grasps things quickly and prefers to verbally communicate ideas quickly may not be as effective for a student who requires visuals and more time to absorb concepts. While peer tutors can be taught the skills to adjust to the learning styles of others, in some cases, another tutor-tutee pairing would be a better match based on their learning styles.
- **Subject area of the class:** Sometimes, a peer tutor realizes that a course area they are assigned to provide support in is not a good fit because they lack knowledge or interest in that area. This can affect the tutor's confidence and effectiveness.

If, for any reason, the student receiving support, the peer tutor, or the classroom educator feels that a pairing needs to be changed, reevaluate the pairing; it likely needs to be changed. It is important to check in regularly with the student receiving support, as they may not independently share concerns about the pairing due to their disability. Through ongoing communication with both the peer tutor and classroom educator, the special educator can monitor the pairing to ensure it remains a good match throughout the school year.

Sometimes, instead of partnering directly with a tutee, a peer tutor is best suited to provide support to the special educator by assisting them in making modifications or accommodations to the curriculum under their direct supervision. Some students are fantastic at this task, which is of particular interest to students who are considering a career in the education field.

What happens if a peer tutor and student do not get along or if the peer isn't providing the needed support?

Make changes as needed. For peer tutor support to be successful, all parties need to be content. If the peers cannot resolve differences, then pair the student with a different peer tutor. If one student in the pair prefers not to be reassigned, then share the benefits of finding a different match that may be more effective for both students. The focus remains on how the change supports everyone. For example, if there is a personality difference that negatively impacts support effectiveness, you can explain that another student who shares similar interests and strengths may be a better fit.

If the peer tutor is not providing adequate support to the student despite training and multiple attempts at guidance, then reassign the pair. If appropriate, you can reassign the peer tutor to a different class and student in hope that it will be a better match. You can also provide additional support and training to the tutor as needed. It is important to meet with the peer tutor to explain how this may affect their grade and remind them of their expected roles and responsibilities. This provides an opportunity for the peer tutor to improve their performance.

If a peer tutor is still not successful at providing support to another student after the reassignment, the peer can help create curricular accommodations and modifications, such as adding adhesive pieces to laminated photos in an adapted matching activity or designing flash cards with visuals with the special educator. They could also serve as a classroom student aide under the educator's direct supervision.

Communication System

Daily communication is critical for the success of everyone involved. Peer tutors provide vital information to the special educator about what is occurring daily in general education classes. Not every peer tutor will have important information to share every single day, but providing space to at least briefly connect builds collaborative relationships. When peer tutors are encouraged to communicate daily with educators (through daily check-ins and daily update forms) and when the teacher and the forms ask them about how the day went and what they need, peer tutors are held accountable and supported.

After pairing students, provide the tutor with a peer tutor folder that has the following information. (Visit **go.SolutionTree.com/specialneeds** to access free downloadable versions of the following forms.)

- Successful learning strategies for that particular student
- Specific skills that the peer tutor can support the student with
- Suggestions on how to best support the student
- Adapted curriculum for the day or week
- Forms that the peer tutor is required to complete
    - "Daily Journal" (page 75)
    - "Homework Log" (page 77)
    - "Daily Update" (page 78)

For example, figure 3.3 (page 62) illustrates the peer tutor support strategies provided to Steven's peer tutor for his clay art class. Steven is a student who has many support needs. He is blind and is working on many skills throughout his day, such as orientation and mobility, including using a cane more effectively so that he can move around his surroundings with increased independence.

I have learned so much about interacting with other people and ways to talk to others. I learned it is about talking with people, not at people, and being patient and not raising your voice when you get frustrated. It is about showing others you are there to help and knowing you are trying to reach a final goal together.

—Peer tutor

Notice that the student's disability label is not included on the information sheet, as this is confidential and does not aid the peer tutor in providing support. Confidentiality is a legal and dignity issue stipulated in FERPA (1974) and other privacy laws, so the peer tutor is not given any confidential information. However, for the peer tutor to be effective, it is important for them to know what they should be *doing* to support the student.

Also included in the peer tutor folders are journals that peer tutors are required to record in daily. Figure 3.4 (page 63) provides an example of a journal completed by one of Steven's peer tutors.

Create a journal that not only provides the special education teacher with useful information but also reminds the peer tutor daily of what they should support the student to accomplish. The journal also serves as a means of accountability for the peer tutor. You can use the reproducible "Daily Journal" (page 75) as is or customize it to meet student needs and communicate in a variety of ways, such as by adding a section for daily homework. However, always follow FERPA (1974) and other applicable privacy laws to maintain student confidentiality and dignity.

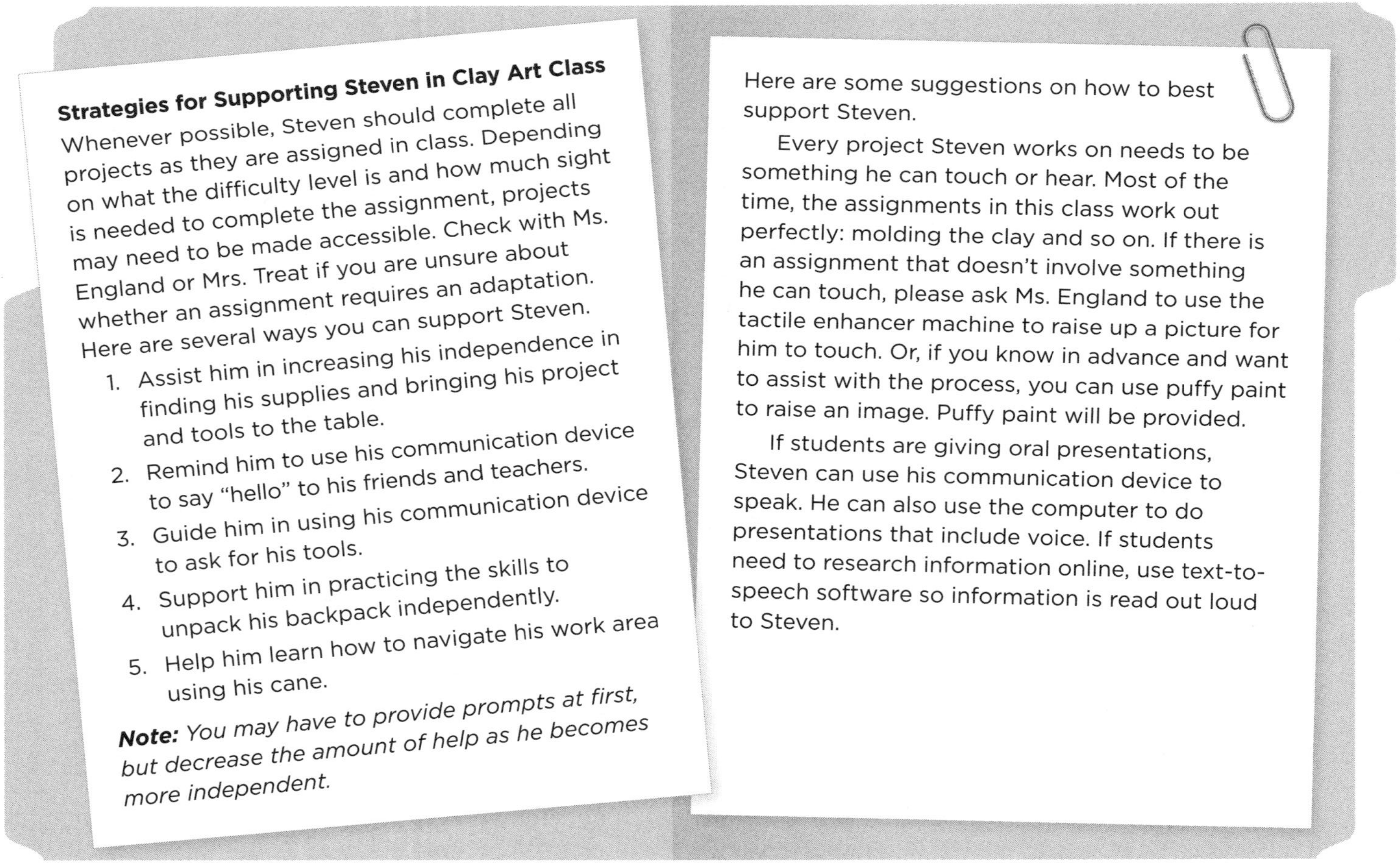

Strategies for Supporting Steven in Clay Art Class

Whenever possible, Steven should complete all projects as they are assigned in class. Depending on what the difficulty level is and how much sight is needed to complete the assignment, projects may need to be made accessible. Check with Ms. England or Mrs. Treat if you are unsure about whether an assignment requires an adaptation. Here are several ways you can support Steven.

1. Assist him in increasing his independence in finding his supplies and bringing his project and tools to the table.
2. Remind him to use his communication device to say "hello" to his friends and teachers.
3. Guide him in using his communication device to ask for his tools.
4. Support him in practicing the skills to unpack his backpack independently.
5. Help him learn how to navigate his work area using his cane.

Note: *You may have to provide prompts at first, but decrease the amount of help as he becomes more independent.*

Here are some suggestions on how to best support Steven.

Every project Steven works on needs to be something he can touch or hear. Most of the time, the assignments in this class work out perfectly: molding the clay and so on. If there is an assignment that doesn't involve something he can touch, please ask Ms. England to use the tactile enhancer machine to raise up a picture for him to touch. Or, if you know in advance and want to assist with the process, you can use puffy paint to raise an image. Puffy paint will be provided.

If students are giving oral presentations, Steven can use his communication device to speak. He can also use the computer to do presentations that include voice. If students need to research information online, use text-to-speech software so information is read out loud to Steven.

Figure 3.3: *Sample of peer tutor support strategies for a specific imaginary student.*

Name: Krista Student supported: Steven

+ = student had an opportunity to work on this activity

− = student did not have an opportunity to work on this activity

	Participated in Group Activities	Worked on Classroom Assignments	Interacted With Others	Used Communication Device to Ask for Tools	Located His Drawer	Used Cane With Increased Independence	A Brief Description of What Happened in Class and Successful Experiences
Monday Feb 8	+	+	+	+	+	+	Steven started his coil pot today. He used his communication device to ask for his tools, but I needed to show him which button to push.
Tuesday Feb 9	+	+	+	+	+	+	Steven continued to work on his coil pot. He found his drawer by himself; I just needed to tell him to go a little to the left!
Wednesday Feb 10	+	+	+	+	+	+	He worked on his coil pot again. He is getting really good about rolling out the clay the way Mrs. Treat showed him.
Thursday Feb 11	+	+	+	+	+	+	Steven finished his coil pot today. He also used his communication device (all by himself) to say "hello" to Erin after she said "hello" to him.
Friday Feb 12	+	+	+	−	−	+	Mrs. Treat explained the artist's report, and we began to research in the library.

Discovery: Answer one or more of the following questions in your response.

What did you learn this week as a peer tutor?

How did you help make an assignment or activity more accessible?

What teaching strategies did you use?

How did you engage the student in classroom activities?

Overall, how is the student doing in class?

I learned that Steven is able to do a lot more on his own than I thought. He is able to roll out the clay all by himself; he just needs a little help putting it into the shape of a pot. Steven is much better about using his communication device. I think we should put more messages on it. I need help figuring out how Steven can do the oral report about his artist.

Figure 3.4: *Example daily journal.*

Peer tutors write in the journal form daily, indicating whether the student they are supporting had an opportunity to work on the skills or activities they are focusing on. This knowledge is important for the special educator because it allows them to identify when a student is not receiving the anticipated opportunities to be engaged academically and socially or not practicing the targeted skills. The first three activities listed on Steven's peer tutor's daily journal pertain to things that all students might be working on, such as participating in class, completing classroom assignments, and interacting with other students. The next three activities are more specific to Steven; they relate to his increased independence in mobility and communication during tasks that are embedded into his routine in the general education class. Note that peer tutors do not collect actual data on a student's progress; they merely indicate which activities the student has had an opportunity to work on.

In addition to their daily entries, peer tutors are expected to respond to one or more of the following discovery questions at the end of the week.

- What did you learn this week as a peer tutor?
- How did you help make an assignment or activity more accessible?
- What teaching strategies did you use?
- How did you engage the student in classroom activities?
- Overall, how is the student doing in class?

These questions make the peer tutor accountable for the support they provide. Because of that, peer tutors tend to recognize the importance of their role and take pride in their work helping others. In addition, peer tutors' responses to these questions provide educators with information that helps them determine both how the peer tutor is providing support (such as the strategies they are implementing and their efforts to engage the student) and how the student is doing, from the peer tutor's perspective.

Peer tutors can keep journals inside their folder in, for example, a bin in the classroom where they sign in daily. After signing in, peer tutors pick up their folder and take it to class with them. When they return from the general education class, five minutes prior to the bell ringing, they place their peer tutor folder back in the bin. This allows the teacher to have access to the journals at any point during the school day if they need any of the information written in the journal. The peer tutor should also use the folder to store homework logs, updates, class notes, and handouts. While this system works well and bundles items in the peer tutor folder, peer tutors can use a digital form of the journal instead.

The teacher overseeing the peer tutors can put information or any adapted curriculum in the peer tutors' folders. Many peer tutors also keep a homework log (see "Homework Log," page 77) in their journal as well. This helps them keep track of what occurs in class and serves as a note-taking tool for them to share with the special educator. We also encourage tutored students to use one and keep it in their own folders.

While the forms do provide an excellent means of communication, daily in-person interactions between the peer tutor and special educator are still necessary. When peer tutors sign in at the beginning of the period or block and when they return with their peer tutor folders at the end are great times to discuss any needed information, materials, or support. If multiple peer tutors need to speak directly with the special educator at the end of a class period, but there is not enough time for the special educator to speak to everyone, tutors can complete a daily update (see "Daily Update," page 78) and leave it for the teacher in a designated area. Peer tutors only need to complete this form if they are unable to communicate directly with the educator and have something pertinent to share that day.

Some educators may prefer peer tutors to complete this daily update digitally, such as through a Google Form. This can be helpful if a peer tutor needs to rush to their next class and requires the flexibility to complete the form later in the day. For example, a peer tutor may need to let the special educator know an exam date has changed, an extensive homework assignment was given, or an upcoming novel needs to be adapted to ensure accessibility. Peer tutors are told during the first training session to report urgent information—such as a health or safety concern—immediately, in person, to the nearest general or special educator.

In most cases, students with disabilities remain in class until the bell rings and independently go to their next class. In those instances, the peer tutor leaves the general education class alone to return their folder and communicate with the special educator. However, some tutored students need assistance navigating to and from their classes, so the tutor and tutee might leave just a few minutes before the end of the class to return to the teacher of record together.

It is important for communication among professionals to extend to all educators involved in a student's learning. This is especially true in special education. It is not unusual for students with disabilities to have several people involved in their education and the implementation of their IEP goals. When a peer tutor becomes part of the support system of students with disabilities, it is important that *any* professional working with the student also has contact with the peer tutor. This could involve a speech-language pathologist educating a peer tutor on communication strategies for a particular class or an orientation and mobility specialist providing instruction to a peer tutor on how to support a student using a cane, for instance. The special educators coordinate with related service providers to schedule times during the school day for providers to collaborate with both general educators and peer tutors. Successful inclusive education depends on all people who work with and support a student communicating effectively with one another.

What about confidentiality issues in regard to what the peer tutor knows about the student with a disability?

Confidential information needs to remain confidential. Therefore, educators must be sensitive about what they share with peer tutors. *Do not* share disability information or IEP content unless both the educator and the family feel it is beneficial to do so. What educators share with the peer tutor is the type of support they should provide. This support includes a variety of ways the peer tutor can help the student, including both general and specific accommodation strategies that would benefit the student, such as verbal prompting or modeling. In general, you can share any skills the student is currently working on.

Attendance System

A daily attendance system that functions smoothly minimizes extra work that would otherwise take away from instructional time. Special educators could take attendance for up to twenty peer tutors each period or block of the school day. It is important to create a user-friendly system for daily attendance that the teacher can easily use. The teacher of record can place a sign-in sheet at an ideal location in the classroom. For example, they might post the sign-in sheet near their desk so the teacher knows who is in attendance.

After students check themselves in, they can quickly greet the teacher and leave for their assigned general education class, unless a more in-depth conversation is needed. Some peer tutors will meet the student they support in the general education classroom; others will walk with the student they support. After about ten minutes maximum, all peer tutors will have signed in, and the teacher can quickly scan the sign-in sheet to confirm who is absent. Paraprofessionals can assist to ensure that all peer tutors check in and that substitute peer tutors are sent to class, as needed.

If a peer tutor is absent, the teacher of record has two choices.

1. Send a substitute peer tutor in place of any absent peer tutor.
2. Contact the general education teacher, if needed, to discuss support options for the student with a disability attending independently. Using a natural support (another student enrolled in that class) for one day is often a great option.

A student may be working on fading their peer support and increasing their independence, so a peer tutor's absence might be the perfect time to give the student a little more independence.

A peer tutor who has been assigned to assist the special educator throughout the school day (such as by making simple accommodations under the educator's direction) rather than support a student in a general education class can also serve as a substitute peer tutor. A substitute peer tutor attends a class and provides support when the regularly assigned peer tutor is absent. Also, if a student with a disability is absent, then that student's peer tutor can serve as a substitute for another student on that day.

To eliminate the possibility of peer tutors signing in and not going to class or having another student sign them in when they are absent, general educators should contact the special educator if a peer tutor does not show up for that period. General educators know that the regular peer tutor or a substitute will attend daily, unless the special educator notifies them otherwise.

Class Assignments

Trying to keep up with all of the general education classwork and activities that peer tutors and tutees share with the special educator can be overwhelming. Set up a well-organized system for students to keep track of graded and in-progress assignments. Peer tutors can provide great support in this area.

For some students, the verbal prompts from the peer tutor reminding them to keep their work in their backpack in specified folders are enough. For other students, storing their work in a portfolio folder in a bin the special educator keeps can be useful. The peer tutor role can include helping a student file their work every day upon their return from the general education class. This will save time on the following day, when the peer tutor, the educator, and the student with a disability will all look for the assignments or activities needed for the day.

It is important to note, however, that while the special educator may assist with collaborative grading, the student should give all completed work to the general educator for grading prior to filing it in any bins or folders. Graded work and work in progress can be kept either with the student or, if the teacher indicates it, with the special educator in a portfolio folder in a bin.

Identify a system for organizing work in progress and graded work that aligns best with the teacher of record's organizational style and students' needs. Whatever you decide, the organization system must work for the teacher of record.

Scheduling

Creatively designing paraprofessionals' schedules, being intentional with students' class schedules, and using peer tutors in differing capacities can make a world of a difference! Figure 3.5 is an example of a schedule. Consider when paraprofessionals' break and lunch times are assigned to maximize support for students. Work closely with the counselors to design ideal class schedules for students, allowing paraprofessionals to easily be spread across the classes that need the most support. Also, a paraprofessional may only be present for the beginning of class, and then a peer tutor can provide the support themselves. Also, a peer tutor can walk a student to a class, ensure the student understands the class activities for the day, and then leave to go to another class to support a different student.

How can we balance all the responsibilities of implementing a peer tutoring course?

Create an organization system that works best for you! Develop a student pairing system, attendance system, and communication system that are easy to use within the structure of your school. Delegate roles to paraprofessionals and peer tutors and ensure everyone understands their roles.

SUMMARY

This chapter outlined the essential steps educators need to take to implement a peer tutoring course at the high school level, including how to gain administrative support and develop the structure of the course. It also offered practical suggestions for successfully launching the program. The next chapter builds on this foundation by presenting examples of what the peer tutoring course curriculum might include, highlighting the topics to cover, student assignments, and engaging activities designed to enhance the learning experience.

Tutored Student	**Period 1** 8:00–8:50 a.m.	**Period 2** 9:00–9:50 a.m.	**Period 3** 10:05–10:55 a.m.	**Period 4** 11:05–11:55 a.m.	**Period 5** 12:35–1:25 p.m.	**Period 6** 1:35–2:25 p.m.
Tanner	**Biology** Room: 201 Peer tutor: Trent	**English** Room: 110 Peer tutor: Siobhan	**Weights** Room: Weight room Peer tutor: Christian	**Art** Room: 515 Peer tutor: Sam	**Math** Room: 404 Peer tutor: Jayne	**History** Room: 330 Peer tutor: Brody
Kiara	**Yoga** Room: Rec room Peer tutor: Tara	**History** Room: 316 Peer tutor: Anderson	**English** Room: 107 Peer tutor: Araceli	**Math** Room: 444 Peer tutor: Aarys	**Choir** Room: 507 Peer tutor: Daniel	**Biology** Room: 204 Peer tutor: Colby
Elena	**Earth Science** Room: 212 Peer tutor: Scarlett	**Math** Room: 414 Peer tutor: Brooke	**Team Sports** Room: Gym Peer tutor: Genevieve	**Geography** Room: 312 Peer tutor: Jackson	**Photography** Room: 502 Peer tutor: Nico	**English** Room: 101 Peer tutor: Sama
Yonan	**Math** Room: 407 Para: Ms. Jobin Peer tutor: Sage	**Geography** Room: 314 Para: Ms. Griffin Peer tutor: Molly	**Theater** Room: Theater Para: None needed Peer tutor: Julian	**English** Room: 115 Para: Ms. Griffin Peer tutor: Riley	**Earth Science** Room: 216 Para: Ms. Jobin Peer tutor: Chris	**Racket Sports** Room: Tennis courts Para: Mr. Chavez Peer tutor: Avalon

Figure 3.5: *Example peer tutor schedule.*

PEER TUTOR EVALUATION FORM

Date: ____________ Class: __________________ Teacher: __________________

We supervise many peer tutors who provide support to students with disabilities in general education classrooms. As you can imagine, it can be difficult to always know how each of them is doing. Therefore, we rely on your input to let us know how peer tutors are doing in your class so that we can instruct them on how to provide better support if needed. If a peer tutor is not being helpful, please discuss this with them and provide guidance as needed. Please let us know as well.

Peer tutors are in your class to support you in meeting the needs of students with disabilities. Please supervise and provide instruction to peer tutors as needed.

Please provide your input as to how __________________________ is doing in

supporting __________________________ in your class.

Return to __________________________. Thank you!

	Always 8–10	**Most Times 6–7**	**Sometimes 4–5**	**Rarely 1–3**	**Never 0**
Punctual (arriving at or near the beginning of class and present until the last five minutes)					
Attentive (focused on class material and the student)					
Respectful (courteous to students and teachers)					
Well behaved (cooperative and not disruptive in class)					
Willing to help (proactive and responsive to the student's needs)					

	Always 8–10	Most Times 6–7	Sometimes 4–5	Rarely 1–3	Never 0
Communicative with the teacher when clarification is needed (proactive in asking the teacher for help to understand expectations)					
Supportive of and helpful to the student (beneficial to the student in class, and only as much as needed)					
Useful to the teacher (willing to follow through with the teacher's instructions)					
Totals					

Additional comments:

SELF-EVALUATION FORM

Date: ____________________

Peer tutor name: ____

Tutored student: ____

Complete the following evaluation form to evaluate yourself as a peer tutor. For each assertion, put a checkmark in the column that applies to your actions. This will help you determine the quality of support you provide and the areas where you can make positive changes.

	I Am Doing Great	**I Am Doing OK**	**I Want to Improve**
I am there every day that I am expected to be.			
I respond to my tutee's needs during class time or as soon as a need is realized.			
I understand what I should do as a peer tutor, and I do it.			
My attitude toward the student, class, and teachers is positive.			
I support the tutee to complete and turn in all assignments, helping only as much as needed.			
I communicate with teachers when the tutee needs more help.			
I remain focused on the student and the class material being used during class time.			
I actively help involve the student in class discussions, group activities, or projects.			

page 1 of 2

In addition to the classroom and special education teachers communicating with me, I also regularly initiate communication with them as needed.			
I ask for help when I need it.			
I listen and respond to the tutee.			
I am a positive role model, showing compassion and respect for everyone.			
I complete my journal and any other assignments daily.			

Count the number of check marks in each column for an overall assessment.

_______: I am doing great.

_______: I am doing OK.

_______: I want to improve.

Comments:

PEER TUTOR SURVEY

Please complete this survey. The information you provide helps us determine which student you will be paired with. (Attach an extra sheet of paper for more writing space if needed.)

Name:		
Date:	Period:	Grade:
*List your current class schedule for this semester on the back of this page. Include period number, class title, and teacher name.		
List the extracurricular activities you are involved in (clubs, sports, faith-based groups, and others).		
List your favorite classes and the reasons you enjoyed them. Be specific.		
List your interests and any hobbies, special talents, and personal strengths.		
List the languages you speak, including sign language.		
Explain why you signed up to be a peer tutor.		
Describe your personal experiences with people with disabilities.		
Share any questions or concerns that you have about being a peer tutor.		

Thank you for signing up to be a peer tutor! We'll let you know at the next class meeting which student you'll be paired with.

DAILY JOURNAL

You are responsible for completing this form every day that you tutor. Keep the completed forms in your folder. The special educator will review them at the end of the week. If you need to communicate something to the special educator sooner, please fill out the daily update form and give it to your teacher on the day of your concern.

Your teacher will indicate points at the end of each week.

- Points for Attendance/Journal are based on your attendance and daily journal completion.
- Points for Communication are based on how effectively you communicate with the teachers you work with.
- Points for Conduct are based on how well you conduct yourself as a peer tutor that week (such as being effective and on task).
- Total points indicate all of these earned points.

Name: ______________________________ Attendance or journal: ______

Student supported: ______________________________ Communication: ______

Conduct: ______

Place a + or – in each column in the following table. Total: ______

+ = student had an opportunity to work on this activity

– = student did not have an opportunity to work on this activity

							A Brief Description of What Happened in Class and Successful Experiences
Monday Date:							
Tuesday Date:							
Wednesday Date:							
Thursday Date:							
Friday Date:							

Discovery: Answer one or more of the following questions below.

What did you learn this week as a peer tutor?

How did you help make an assignment or activity more accessible?

What teaching strategies did you use?

How did you engage the student in classroom activities?

Overall, how is the student doing in class?

HOMEWORK LOG

Please complete this log on a daily basis and keep it in your folder. This will help you and your tutee keep track of what occurs in class and will serve as a note-taking tool to share with the special educator.

Class:	Period:
Teacher:	
Student:	
Peer tutor:	

Write the dates below the days in the following table.

	Monday ______	**Tuesday** ______	**Wednesday** ______	**Thursday** ______	**Friday** ______
Homework					
Tests or quizzes					
Projects or assignments					
Other notes					

DAILY UPDATE

Please complete this form if you need to communicate something to the teacher in charge and are unable to do so in person at this time. It can be about class assignments, an upcoming test or project, concerns, questions, suggestions, or anything else.

Peer tutor name: ____

Student being supported: ______________________________________

Please share any pertinent information that you want the teacher to know.

Part 2

USING THE PEER TUTORING COURSE CURRICULUM

While peer tutors spend most of their time supporting students with disabilities in general education classes, the teacher of record should first schedule dedicated times to meet with tutors throughout the course. These training sessions help tutors understand special education, inclusive practices, and learning theory. Each school creates and tailors its training sessions and course curriculum to meet the needs of the peer tutors and, often, the students with disabilities as well. The following chapters explain what you need for the seven peer tutoring training sessions, including the activities and materials for each.

- **Chapter 4 (session one):** Inclusive education, peer tutor expectations, and digital portfolio project
- **Chapter 5 (session two):** Support strategies and curriculum accessibility
- **Chapter 6 (session three):** Communication
- **Chapter 7 (session four):** Social inclusion
- **Chapter 8 (session five):** Book talk
- **Chapter 9 (session six):** Research project
- **Chapter 10 (session seven):** Digital portfolio presentations

It is important to be flexible regarding the content of the planned training sessions and to adapt them when necessary. Additionally, the content, activities, and even the number of sessions may change from year to year due to the needs of the changing population of peer tutors and students. For example, it may be that in one particular school year, many students use assistive technology to communicate. Therefore, it could be vital for peer tutors to understand how assistive technology devices work so they are able to communicate with their assigned students and model best communication practices for the other students in the general education classes. In this case, the special educator can arrange for the first training session to include a focus on communication, specifically how to operate the communication devices that students are using.

[The student I tutor] has honestly taught me more in this short period of time than I think I can ever teach her. I haven't been known to be the nicest or the most patient person by my peers; but there is something about her charisma that seems to have brought that side out of me.

—Peer tutor

Peer tutors cannot provide support to students in their classes on training session days. The week before the training session, remind all the general educators who will be impacted so they can plan for alternative support. In addition, remind peer tutors of training dates so they know to attend the session rather than go to their assigned general education classrooms on that day. Prior to the day of the training session, peer tutors can help the general educator find another student in the class (natural support) who would be helpful to the student if any need arises during their absence. The following is an example template.

> *Dear [general education teacher's name],*
>
> *We will conduct a training session on [date of training]. All our peer tutors will attend. Therefore, [name of peer tutor] will not attend your class with [name of tutee] on that day. Please arrange alternative support in your classroom for that day and let us know if you need additional support from the special education department.*
>
> *These training sessions, which we hold several times throughout the school year, allow us to provide much-needed guidance and training for tutors so they can give the best possible support to students. Thank you so much for your assistance with this.*

Peer tutor training sessions can be scheduled in a variety of ways, always based on what is best for educators and students. One possible option is to offer the training sessions during each class period on a single day. For example, you could dedicate every Monday during the first few weeks of school to a different training topic. Another option is to only provide training for a couple of periods each day (such as period 1 and 2 on Monday, period 3 and 4 on Tuesday, and period 5 and 6 on Wednesday). A new training topic could occur every week, every other week, or every few weeks. Typically, training sessions 1 through 4 are provided early in the school year or semester. You can hold training sessions 5 through 7 during the second half of the course.

Plan training sessions on days and times that are optimal for both educators' and students' schedules. This is where paraprofessionals or on-site substitute teachers can be very helpful. If all students with disabilities are included in general education classrooms, the educator will be available to provide these trainings. However, if some students are not included in general education classes during periods when the training sessions will take place, consider assigning a paraprofessional to work with them or having the students with disabilities participate in the trainings. Students can help present the information or participate in activities with the peer tutors.

Due to the popularity of the course, peer tutoring enrollment often includes many returning peer tutors who have already attended the training sessions and completed the activities. Therefore, consider adding components to the training sessions that address these returning students' needs. For example, provide extension activities that build on the training they received previously, or assign co-teaching responsibility during training sessions, allowing them to teach certain sections of the session that they have already mastered and are comfortable teaching.

By remaining flexible and open to change when implementing the curriculum, you can meet all peer tutors' unique needs. The better you support and train peer tutors, the better they can support tutees. This, in turn, enhances the education of students with disabilities. The reproducible "Peer Tutor Training Sessions at a Glance" (page 34) provides a bird's-eye view of all the lesson plans.

CHAPTER 4

Session One: Inclusive Education, Peer Tutor Expectations, and Digital Portfolio Project

This training session provides peer tutors with background information on diversity, respectful language, and inclusive education. It also addresses broader ideas, such as how the concept of inclusion relates to students' neighborhood community and to society as a whole. In addition, the session includes tips for successful peer tutoring and an introduction to the digital portfolio project, which is a final, comprehensive project. While each training session is intended to be completed in a single class period, session one has numerous activities, so it may not be possible to finish them all in one period. Therefore, educators can either select specific activities to cover during one session or provide activities over the course of two days.

The student learning objective for session one: Students will gain an understanding of what inclusive education is, what the responsibilities and expectations of peer tutors are, and how to speak and write using respectful language.

You will need the following materials.

- Boxes of assorted cream chocolates
- Reproducible "Benefits of Inclusive Education" (page 95)
- Reproducible "Tips for Being a Successful Peer Tutor" (page 96)
- Reproducible "Respect" (page 97)

- Reproducible "Person-First and Identity-First Language" (page 98)
- Reproducible "Digital Portfolio Project" (page 99)
- Reproducible "Digital Portfolio Project Rubric" (page 102)

LIFE-IS-SWEETER-WITH-CHOCOLATE ACTIVITY

This ten-minute activity, adapted from Leah Katz, Caren Sax, and Douglas Fisher (2003), is an icebreaker to draw attention to the course's core tenets, which emphasize that each person is unique, disability does not define a person, and human differences should be valued. Buy boxes of chocolates in advance so that each student has one piece of chocolate. Take care to purchase chocolates whose filling is not easy to determine. Creams are ideal! And, as always, be mindful of any allergies that students might have.

1. Before handing out candy, let everyone know that they should *not* bite into their chocolate.
2. Allow each student to choose one piece from an assortment of chocolates.
3. Ask students to turn to the person next to them and predict what flavor is inside their own piece of chocolate.
4. After their predictions, tell the students to take a bite of their chocolate; then, ask, "How many of you made the correct prediction?" In general, very few (if any) will have guessed correctly.
5. Ask, "What does this tell us?" Typically, students arrive at the conclusion that just as we don't know what a piece of chocolate is by merely looking at it, we can't tell what a person is like simply by looking at them. This discussion can go even further with the idea that knowing what a person's disability is does not tell us what that person is truly like.
6. End by clarifying that nothing takes the place of really getting to know someone. You might have a student with a disability conduct this part of the training session. Doing so highlights their uniqueness and shows the tutors that even if they know the student has Down syndrome or autism, for instance, that does not mean they know anything about who they are.

INTRODUCTION TO INCLUSIVE EDUCATION

Now that students are focused on the ideas that human differences are valuable and that disabilities don't define a person, you can introduce the topic of inclusive education. In the context of education for students with disabilities, the term *inclusion* should not be politicized; it refers to a research-based practice focused on ensuring access to an equitable education. Inclusive education is mandated in U.S. federal law and has positive academic and social outcomes for students with and without disabilities (Hehir et al., 2016). Incorrectly framing inclusion as a political concept takes away from its purpose: providing appropriate supports and services so students with disabilities can learn alongside their peers to the maximum extent possible.

1. Begin the discussion by asking students if they can explain the meaning of *inclusion*, encouraging them to consider all areas of life, not just education. Start by asking, "What does inclusion for students with disabilities look like at a school?" Responses should include going to the same classes as other students, participating in group activities in the classroom, attending school assemblies and other functions during the school day, eating lunch with peers in common areas, and attending after-school events, such as football games or club events. Students will undoubtedly come up with even more responses.
2. Next, ask, "What does inclusion look like for individuals with disabilities in the community?" This can include going to common places like grocery stores and restaurants. It can also include attending fun events and visiting places that have been carefully designed so that all can enjoy them, such as theme parks with rides that are wheelchair accessible, movie theaters that provide closed captioning for people who are deaf, and playgrounds and museums set up for those with sensory issues.
3. Once students have a good sense of what inclusion looks like in schools and in the community, ask them to take several minutes to think about their personal educational experiences. Have them reflect on the location where students with disabilities were taught when they were in elementary, middle, and high school.
    - Were they at the same school?
    - Were they in the same building?
    - Were they in the same classroom?
    - If not, where were they?

    Have the students share their answers with a shoulder buddy and then the whole class. Great discussions typically evolve, and the thought-provoking responses students have are amazing!

4. Wrap up this part of the discussion by letting them know that in the past, special education was considered a *place*, determining which schools and classes students with disabilities attended. Now, special education is viewed not as a place but as a *service* provided to students with disabilities, alongside their peers, in general education classrooms.
5. Let the students know the way inclusive education works at your school and the important role peer tutors play in creating successful inclusive opportunities at their school.

Frequently Asked Questions

Does *inclusive education* refer to all students with disabilities, including those with mild and moderate support needs (specific learning disabilities) as well as extensive support needs (intellectual and developmental disabilities)?

Yes. Not only is it the law in the United States to provide the least restrictive environment to all students (IDEA, 2004), but there are also many benefits. We share those benefits in the upcoming section.

When selecting general education classes for students with disabilities, are only electives (such as art, theater, or music) considered?

No. All classes, including core academic classes, should be options. When the appropriate supports are provided—curricular adaptations, peer supports, and assistive technologies—even students with extensive support needs can be successful in academic classes (Pineda Zapata & Brooks, 2017).

BENEFITS OF INCLUSIVE EDUCATION

Now that students have had the opportunity to form their own understanding of what inclusion is, you can introduce the benefits of inclusive education using the following activity.

1. Have students get into groups of three or four.
2. Ask half of the students to come up with as many benefits as they can think of that inclusive education has for students *with* disabilities. Students can write each of their ideas on sticky notes.
3. Ask the other half of the class to do the same for the benefits that inclusive education has for students *without* disabilities. Encourage the

students to brainstorm as many benefits as they can, and challenge them to see which group can come up with the most benefits.

4. While students are working on this, draw a Venn diagram on chart paper or a whiteboard that looks like the one in figure 4.1.

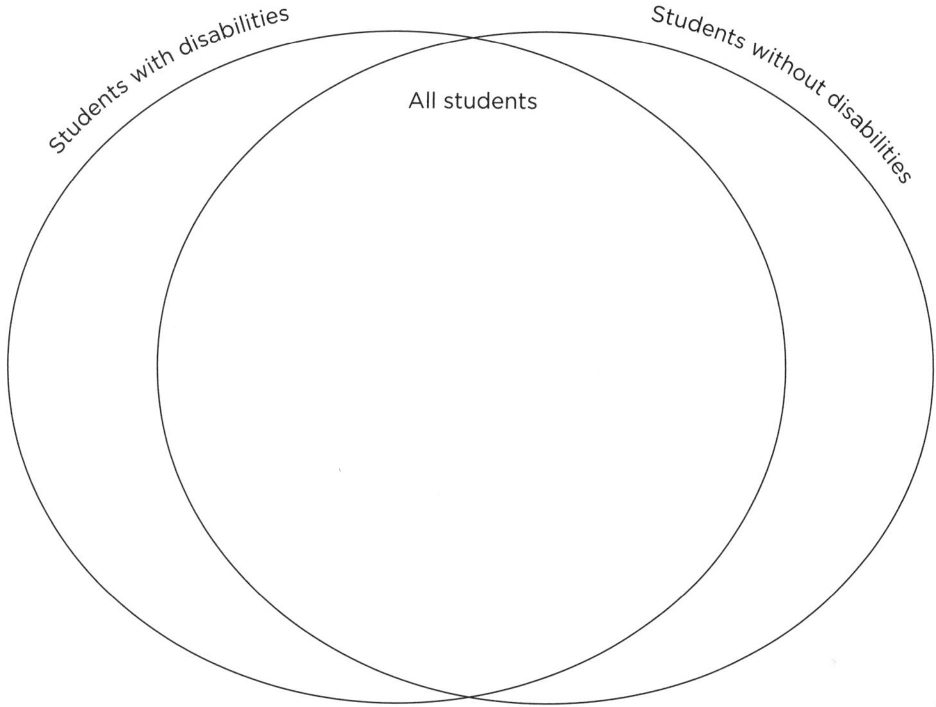

Figure 4.1: *Benefits of inclusive education Venn diagram.*

5. Once students have completed their sticky notes, have them put them on their assigned section of the Venn diagram displayed in the front of the room (on a whiteboard or on chart paper).
6. Pass out the reproducible "Benefits of Inclusive Education" (page 95) so that each student can fill out their copy during the following discussion.
7. Read aloud to the class each sticky note and decide collectively whether it would actually be beneficial to both groups. If so, put the sticky note in the middle portion of the diagram. As you decide placement for each sticky note, instruct students to write it on their Venn diagram.

Throughout the discussion and activity, it should become apparent to everyone that inclusive education has numerous benefits for all students. Figure 4.2 (page 88) provides a list of benefits to help guide the discussion.

Students With Disabilities	Students Without Disabilities	All Students
• More opportunities for communication, social interactions, and friendships • Active participation in the school community • Equal access to all curricula and activities • Increase in academic skills • Participation in an environment that reflects mainstream society	• Opportunities to embrace diversity • More appreciation for and acceptance of human differences • A better understanding and more respect for individuals who learn and communicate differently • Development of ideas and strategies to create inclusive communities	• Improvement in social skills • Opportunities to teach and learn from peers • An education in an environment that supports and respects everyone • Improvement in self-esteem • Formation of new friendships • Development of community and connections

Figure 4.2: *Benefits of inclusive education talking points.*

Visit ***go.SolutionTree.com/specialneeds*** *for a free reproducible version of this figure.*

RESPONSIBILITIES AND EXPECTATIONS OF PEER TUTORS

As a result of the previous activities in this session, peer tutors will have developed an awareness of how important and truly beneficial inclusion is for all. It is now time for them to learn more about their role in making inclusion the best it can be.

1. Pass out the reproducibles "Tips for Being a Successful Peer Tutor" (page 96) and "Respect" (page 97). The first handout provides tips that guide peers in gaining an understanding of the roles and expectations of peer tutors.
2. Ask for a student volunteer to read the first tip aloud. Then, ask the whole class why this tip is important and what the possible consequences are if it is not followed.
3. Once there is some consensus from the group on the importance of this tip, move on to the next tip and hold a similar discussion about each tip on the handout.
4. When the class has discussed all thirteen tips, use a think-pair-share to discuss the question "Which one of these tips do you feel is most

important, and why?" Students first think on their own and then pair up with a student to discuss their thoughts.

5. Lead a discussion by having one person from each pair share their responses with the whole class.

The next part of this training session reviews the reproducible "Respect" (page 97). One way that respect is expressed is through prosocial behavior. Students' prosocial behavior positively impacts both themselves and the students around them. Prosocial behavior leads to similar behavior in peers and is "positively associated with [students'] cognitive, behavioral, and affective engagement" (Brass et al., 2024, p. 2795). Another key point is that while both educators and students value respect, they differ in how they show respect, which may be due to developmental, cultural, and generational differences (Audley & Jović, 2020; University of Minnesota Extension, n.d.).

[Peer tutoring] has changed my outlook on people and life.

—Peer tutor

When reviewing the reproducible "Respect," you can follow the same procedure you used with the previous handout: Address all nine tips and discuss the importance of each. Do the same think-pair-share, discussing which point they believe to be most important and why.

During the discussion of these two handouts is a good time to answer questions that peer tutors may have about their role and the expectations. They may also need instruction—and possibly reassurance—regarding their interactions with the students they are working with.

RESPECTFUL LANGUAGE

With a clear understanding of their role as a peer tutor and the ways in which respect can be provided to all students, peer tutors can now dive into what respectful language sounds like. Begin with this lesson, which was adapted from activities by Edmund J. Sass (2015), professor emeritus of education at the College of Saint Benedict. During this training session, discuss language and the extent to which it can influence others' perceptions of the people being talked about. Begin with the following points about often-used terminology.

Write the words *disability*, *handicap*, and *challenged* on the board. Ask students to write which word they would most often use to describe a person. Would they say a person "has a disability," "is handicapped," or "is challenged"? Ask for a show of hands with each option. Then, discuss the meanings of each.

- *Disability* is defined as "a physical or mental impairment that substantially limits one or more major life [activities]" (ADA National Network, n.d.). The word is the generally accepted term, replacing the word *handicapped* in some U.S. federal laws. While this is the preferred terminology as this book goes to press, language evolves over time, and at some point, the word *disability* may become outdated. For example, the word *retarded* used to be part of the clinical classification system for people with disabilities, and its reference to people was considered acceptable. However, its use as a derogatory term has given the word negative connotations. This unfortunately led to a presumption that mental retardation (or the current *intellectual disability*) was a negative condition, and it became deeply offensive to people with disabilities.
- *Handicap* originated from an old English game in which the loser was left with his hand in his cap and was thought to be at a disadvantage (Handicap, n.d.). Using a word with that origin to describe a person with a disability is derogatory. Needless to say, this archaic terminology should not be used to characterize people, as it could evoke negative emotions like pity or fear. However, *handicap* does acceptably capture a disadvantage that occurs for a person (for example, stairs are a *handicap* to a person in a wheelchair). Another example is parking spaces that say *handicapped*, referencing their use for people with disabilities. However, *accessible parking* is a more accurate term (Snow, 2005).
- *Challenged* is often used in place of the word *disability*. However, many people with disabilities don't view themselves as challenged. For example, they may not be able to do certain things because they use a wheelchair, not because they are unable or unwilling to accept a challenge. An additional consideration is that the term *challenged* could be considered a *euphemism*, a word or phrase used as a kinder or gentler way to refer to something unpleasant or embarrassing. Since having a disability should never be viewed as unpleasant or embarrassing, there is no need for a euphemism. Therefore, the word *challenged* can be an insult.

At this point, introduce the differences between person-first and identity-first language.

- *Person-first language* emphasizes the person first, with their disability being just one of the many characteristics of that person. In other words, a disability is what an individual has, not what an individual is.

- *Identity-first language* emphasizes the disability as a core part of a person's identity and reinforces that there is no shame in claiming their disability.

Both are considered acceptable and respectful ways of referring to people with disabilities; it may be just a matter of asking the person what they prefer. Better yet, refer to them by their name! The guidelines for both person-first language and identity-first language are in place for when it is necessary to bring up a person's disability (though it is not always necessary). Table 4.1 provides simple examples of person-first and identity-first language. In addition, the reproducible "Person-First and Identity-First Language" (page 98) contains directions for an activity in which the students can practice using both approaches.

Table 4.1: *Person-First and Identity-First Language Examples*

Person-First Language	Identity-First Language
A person with a disability	A disabled person
A girl with autism	An autistic girl
A girl with a learning disability	The learning-disabled girl
My friend with dysleXia	My dyslexic friend

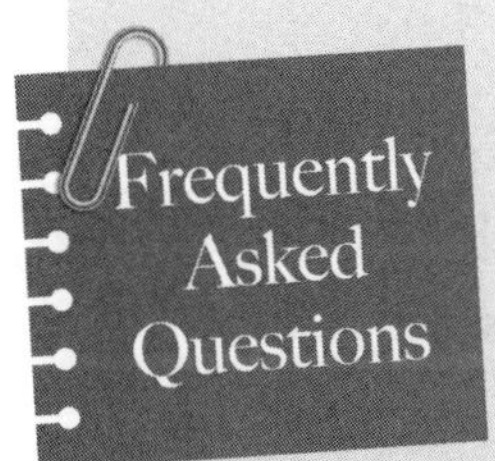

How do you know when to use person-first versus identity-first language?

You don't always know. You may be able to gather clues by observing and listening to how an individual interacts with others and what language they use. You can also consider asking the individual which approach they prefer. If this is not possible, use what feels best for you.

Are there organizations or groups that tend to prefer one approach to language over the other?

Yes. Many people in the autistic community prefer identity-first language over person-first language. The Autistic Self Advocacy Network (ASAN), a grassroots disability-rights organization in the United States for the autistic community, encourages everyone to use identity-first language and believes it is offensive not to do so. The same is true with the Deaf community. These individuals tend to view deafness as a cultural identity, not a disability. On the other hand, people with intellectual or developmental disabilities (and their advocates) tend to use person-first language, as they feel their disability is not central to their identity.

Does language really matter?

Yes, it does. The language we hear, in this case regarding disability, shapes how we think (Boroditsky, 2011). We avoid phrases like "suffers from" or "is inflicted with," as they imply that disability is negative. What matters most is that when we bring up a person's disability, we never present it as something negative, because it is not.

DOT-AND-CIRCLE ACTIVITY

You can now introduce the dot-and-circle activity, adapted from Carol Mauri, Kristi Radetski, and Amie Wong (1995). This activity offers a strong visual representation of how disability is just one aspect of a person. It builds on earlier discussions about using respectful language by helping students understand that there are many other ways to describe and think about a person who has a disability.

1. Draw a large circle on a chalkboard, a whiteboard, or an overhead transparency. Explain that this whole circle represents one person.
2. Ask a student to name the fictitious person. Once they answer, place a dot anywhere in the circle to represent the person's name. Explain that each dot represents one thing about the person.
3. Ask the class how old the person is and place another dot. Continue asking questions about the imaginary person, such as about their personality, sense of humor, hair color, and interests, as well as their favorite hobbies, music genres, school subjects, sports, and movies. Continue until you have at least ten dots, but feel free to put as many dots as you would like.
4. After placing about half of the dots you plan to put in the circle, state to the students, "This person also has a disability" and place another dot in the circle.
5. Continue asking students questions to get to your minimum of ten dots.
6. When you have ten dots or more, state that this person has many wonderful, unique qualities about them, and disability is only one of those qualities. While this person can be described by their disability when it is appropriate to the situation, they can also be characterized by any of their other qualities ("a funny girl," "a boy who loves baseball," or "a great dancer," for instance). Share that it is sometimes the case that

people with disabilities are only identified by—and seen through the lens of—their disability. Instead, we want to make sure we see *all* that is wonderful about a person, not just their disability.

The dot-and-circle visual created on the board is a reference that helps students remember that a person's disability is only one aspect of who they are. Peer tutors have visited educators years later to share that they remember the dot-and-circle activity and that it reminds them to use descriptors other than a person's disability when speaking about them.

This is the last group activity of this session. Students thus far have learned a great deal about an appreciation of differences, inclusive education, respectful language, and their role as a peer tutor. They are now ready to learn about the peer tutor digital portfolio project that they will work on throughout the school year, beginning after the first training session.

PEER TUTOR DIGITAL PORTFOLIO PROJECT

Peer tutors work on their digital portfolio projects throughout the entire school year. This project is a culmination of the experiences the tutor and tutee have and the growth they undergo over the duration of the course. It helps peer tutors understand the needs and skills that are quite important to the student they are supporting.

For the project, students are guided by several writing prompts following each training session. As part of their final grade for the course, peer tutors present their completed portfolios to both the peer tutoring course members and the students they supported. An additional result of this project is that the peer tutor can include this portfolio as part of their existing high school portfolio, which they can share with potential future employers or attach to college or scholarship applications. Of course, parent or guardian permission is required if peer tutors plan to display photographs to outside agencies.

Review the reproducibles "Digital Portfolio Project" (page 99) and "Digital Portfolio Project Rubric" (page 102) with the students. Then, have students create the template for their portfolio on a website, with the eight pages listed here in addition to the title page. Each page of the portfolio (following the cover page) should be titled as follows.

Inclusive Education

Support Strategies and Curriculum Accessibility

Communication

Social Inclusion

Book Talk

Research Project

Final Reflection

Additional Entries

Google Sites are an easy way for each student to create these portfolios. However, first consider exploring whether your school already has a preferred website platform for creating digital portfolios.

HOMEWORK

Assign the first portion of the portfolio—Inclusive Education—to be completed for homework. The prompt listed on students' copy of "Digital Portfolio Project" for session one training is as follows.

Following this training, please upload your copies of "Benefits of Inclusive Education" (completed during the training session) and "Person-First and Identity-First Language" (completed for homework). In addition, write one or two paragraphs explaining at least one thing that is important for the student you are supporting to learn, as well as at least one goal for yourself in this class. Consult an educator if you need help determining what is important for your student to learn. Include ideas for how you will be able to support this student. In addition, please provide two photographs of the student working in their class. (You can also be in the photograph if both you and the student you are working with would like.)

Note that if either the tutee or tutor is uncomfortable having photographs of themselves included in the portfolio, educators should help students come up with alternatives, such as printed images from the internet or copies of completed work.

SUMMARY

The activities and discussions in this first training session provide peer tutors with a strong foundation for understanding inclusion and the peer tutor's roles and responsibilities. After this session, peer tutors may become positive role models to others around them by demonstrating, through both their actions and their words, a true appreciation for human differences and a respect for people with disabilities. While the tips and strategies introduced in this session are fairly general, the next three sessions focus on more-specific support strategies related to curriculum accessibility, communication, and social inclusion.

BENEFITS OF INCLUSIVE EDUCATION

Peer tutors: Complete this form during the discussion following the brainstorming activity. Wait until the class has collectively decided whether a benefit applies to only one of the groups or to both groups before recording it on this form.

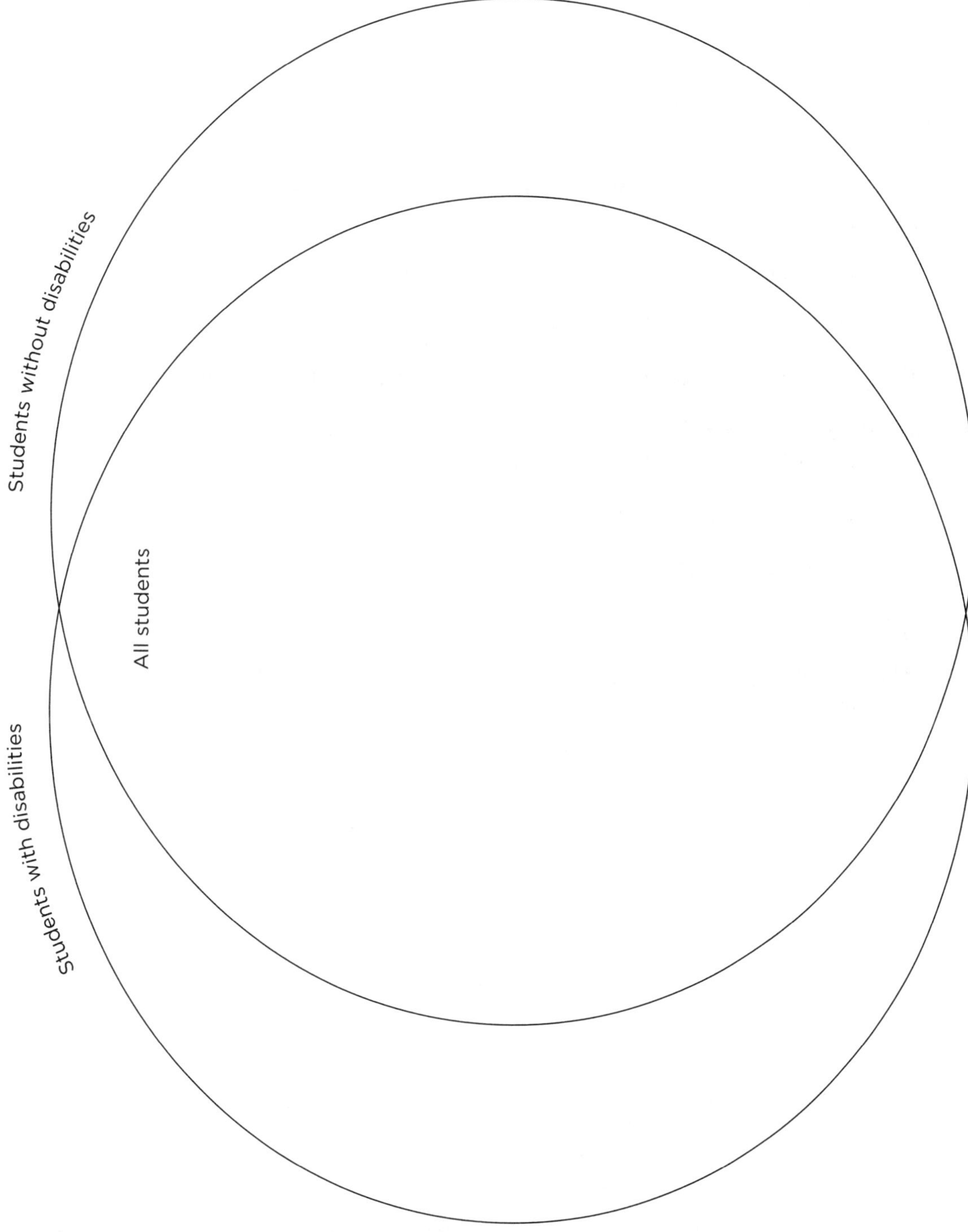

TIPS FOR BEING A SUCCESSFUL PEER TUTOR

Keep the following in mind as you tutor.

Arrive punctually to class on a daily basis.

Respond to the student's needs during class time, as soon as a need is realized.

Determine what you can do to **be supportive and helpful**.

Be respectful and **have a positive attitude** toward the student, class, and teachers.

Support the student to complete and turn in all assignments and communicate with the teachers if your tutee needs more help.

Remain focused on class material and the student.

Follow the classroom rules and **behave appropriately**.

Actively involve the student in class discussions, group activities, and projects.

Initiate communication with the classroom and special education teachers on a regular basis, as needed.

Be an active listener and **respond** to the student as needed.

Be a positive role model by showing compassion and respect for everyone.

Complete your daily journal and any other assignments.

Inform teachers immediately if there are any medical or safety concerns regarding the tutee.

RESPECT

As a peer tutor, you have the opportunity to gain a better understanding of issues concerning individuals with disabilities. You will discover that although people with disabilities may learn differently, they still have some of the same qualities and interests as you and your friends.

You can be respectful toward others in many ways. Simply stated, you should treat everyone the way you want to be treated. As a peer tutor, you are in a position to model for other students and teachers that talking with a student who has a disability does not need to be "special" or different than interacting with anyone else. As you interact with a student you support, others will see the respect you show toward the student and, in turn, will have a better appreciation for human differences.

Here are some tips on how to show respect to the student you support.

Recognize that the student you support is similar in age to you, so treat them as you would anyone your age.
Allow the student the opportunity to complete classwork on their own first, rather than assuming they always need your help.
Always explain how you are going to help the student before providing them with support.
Focus on what the student's positive qualities and skills are, not on what they can't do.
Use respectful language when talking about a person with a disability.
Don't speak for the student. Allow them to communicate themselves.
Talk *with* the student rather than *about* them. For example, instead of just telling a classmate that the tutee doesn't like a particular task, help the tutee communicate this to the classmate.
Respect the student's confidentiality. Do not talk to others about them. If others try to engage you in a confidential conversation about the student, you might say, "I want to respect their privacy, so I'd rather not talk about it."
Celebrate the successes that you and the tutee experience. You are both making a difference!

Source: Adapted from Villalobos, P. (n.d.). Peer tutor resource manual *[Unpublished manuscript]. San Diego State University Interwork Institute.*

PERSON-FIRST AND IDENTITY-FIRST LANGUAGE

While both person-first language and identity-first language are considered acceptable and respectful ways of referring to people with disabilities, many people have very strong preferences. Therefore, it is important to recognize the differences in each approach. And remember, if you are ever unsure of which approach to use, just ask the person you are referring to what they prefer.

The following sentences refer to someone with a disability. Decide whether person-first or identity-first language is being used. Then, change the wording of the sentence to reflect the other approach. The first one is done for you.

1. The autistic boy is a very good artist.

   Language: *Identity first*

   Rewrite: *The boy with autism is a very good artist.*

2. There is a kid with a disability in my science class.

   Language: ______________________________

   Rewrite: ______________________________

3. Disabled people have rights, just like everyone else.

   Language: ______________________________

   Rewrite: ______________________________

4. I am a peer tutor for a girl who uses a wheelchair.

   Language: ______________________________

   Rewrite: ______________________________

5. My daughter is disabled.

   Language: ______________________________

   Rewrite: ______________________________

6. I heard that Maria is learning disabled.

   Language: ______________________________

   Rewrite: ______________________________

7. The new girl on the cheer team has epilepsy.

   Language: ______________________________

   Rewrite: ______________________________

8. The Down syndrome boy has a great sense of humor.

   Language: ______________________________

   Rewrite: ______________________________

DIGITAL PORTFOLIO PROJECT

Your portfolio project is the culmination of your experiences as well as those of the student you supported during your time as a peer tutor. The project should reflect two things: (1) what you learned from the peer tutor training sessions and (2) what the student you supported learned in their class. It can also include any day-to-day learning you experienced while providing support.

The writing prompts for you to complete after each training session follow. In addition to writing responses to these prompts and including pictures, please create at least five more entries for your portfolio. Demonstrate the impact your support had on the student and highlight their achievements. You might include student work samples, photographs of art projects they made, photographs of the student participating in class activities, positive notes from educators, positive comments other students made, and more. When uploading photographs, please briefly describe what the picture highlights.

For each writing, use the title that precedes the prompt.

Inclusive Education

Following this training, please upload your copies of "Benefits of Inclusive Education" (completed during the training session) and "Person-First and Identity-First Language" (completed for homework). In addition, write one or two paragraphs explaining at least one thing that is important for the student you are supporting to learn, as well as at least one goal for yourself in this class. Consult an educator if you need help determining what is important for your student to learn. Include ideas for how you will be able to support this student. In addition, please provide two photographs of the student working in their class. (You can also be in the photograph if both you and the student you are working with would like.)

Support Strategies and Curriculum Accessibility

Following this training, please ask the classroom teacher for an unadapted assignment from the class you provide support in. Considering any forms of support the student has been receiving and the things you have learned in this training, what teaching strategies, along with any adaptations to increase accessibility, would you suggest? Upload photographs or actual documents of the assignment and write a short paragraph explaining the steps required to make the assignment more accessible for your tutee. In addition, complete the "Levels of Prompting" handout and upload it to your portfolio.

Communication

Following this training, please write two paragraphs about communication. One paragraph should explain the importance of teaching communication skills to students. The second paragraph should explain specific strategies you could use to help the student you work with learn better communication skills. Add two additional photographs to your portfolio that capture people communicating and how communication relates to your role as a peer tutor. Examples of photographs to use could include students using communication devices, interacting in cooperative group learning activities, or participating in class presentations.

Social Inclusion

Following this training, please complete the handout "Strategies for Facilitating Social Interactions." Provide examples of strategies you could use to increase social interactions for the student you are working with. An example of how to complete this assignment is given in the handout "Strategies for Facilitating Social Interactions—Example Student Amari." Add two additional photographs to your portfolio that capture what facilitating social interactions looks like and how it relates to your role as a peer tutor. Examples of photographs to use include social activities and interactions, both in and out of the classroom.

Book Talk

This is assigned during the second half of the course.

Please answer the questions about the novel your teacher assigned to you by the due date. Following the class discussion, add any insights you gained from it to your written responses. Then, write one or two paragraphs sharing whether you liked the book, and why or why not. Include in your reflection how the book might apply to you as a peer tutor, to the student you support, or to any other student you know. Upload your written responses to the discussion questions, as well as your reflection, to your digital portfolio.

Research Project

This is assigned during the second half of the course.

Following the prompts on the handout "Research Project," compose a two- or three-page report related to the work you are doing in this class. Once complete, upload the project to your portfolio.

Final Reflection

This is due at the end of the course.

Please write at least two paragraphs describing your experiences as a peer tutor and the ways peer tutoring has affected you. Include positive experiences you and the student you supported had, as well as any challenges that you may have experienced.

Additional Entries

Work on these throughout the duration of the course.

Please provide at least five additional entries in this section. As mentioned in the second paragraph of this handout, these additions could include student work samples, copies of class projects, photographs of projects the student completed with your support, photographs of the student participating in class activities, positive notes from educators or staff, positive comments other students made, or any other materials that add value to your project. Please be sure to check with teachers to confirm the appropriateness of any entries not listed here. When uploading photographs or work samples, please provide a short note describing what they highlight.

DIGITAL PORTFOLIO PROJECT RUBRIC

Student name: ______________________________ Date: ______________

Project Element	Performance Criteria	Comments	Points Earned
Eight sections	• All eight sections (web pages) are included and clearly labeled using the required titles. (8 points) • Most sections are included and clearly labeled using the required titles, with minor omissions or limited detail. (6–7 points) • Multiple required sections are missing or significantly incomplete. (0–5 points)		
Writing pieces and uploads	• All required writing pieces and uploads (handouts, assignments, reflections, photos) are included. (20 points) • Most required writing pieces and uploads (handouts, assignments, reflections, photos) are included, but some are missing. (11–19 points) • Many required writing pieces and uploads (handouts, assignments, reflections, photos) are missing. (0–10 points)		

page 1 of 2

Digital portfolio project appearance	• Design is visually engaging and professional. Layout enhances understanding and interest. Pages are well structured. Content is easy to navigate. (7 points) • Design is visually appealing and organized. Layout is mostly clear. Navigation is functional. (4–6 points) • Design is distracting or cluttered in places. Layout is disorganized. Navigation is confusing. (0–3 points)		
Digital portfolio project presentation	• Shared digital portfolio with strong speaking skills (eye contact, volume, and pacing). (5 points) • Shared digital portfolio with good speaking skills (eye contact, volume, and pacing). (3–4 points) • Shared digital portfolio but lacked effective speaking skills (eye contact, volume, and pacing). (0–2 points)		
Total			

CHAPTER 5

Session Two: Support Strategies and Curriculum Accessibility

Session two provides peer tutors with some specific teaching strategies to implement when working with the student they support. Various levels of prompting will be covered, with an emphasis on the idea that peer tutors should only offer as much prompting as necessary, and always with the goal to fade the support when possible. This session also explores curriculum accessibility and provides the peer tutors with easy accommodations and modifications that they can implement under the supervision of teachers. Students have an opportunity to practice what they learned using case studies and sample assignments.

At first, I felt uncomfortable but now I feel a lot better because I have had the experience [of peer tutoring] and getting to know [students with disabilities].

—Peer tutor

The student learning objective for session two: Students will be able to demonstrate an understanding of how curriculum is made accessible to all students.

You will need the following materials.

- Reproducible "Teaching Strategies and Accommodations" (page 111)
- Reproducible "Student Case Studies for Curriculum Accessibility" (page 114)
- Reproducible "Levels of Prompting" (page 116)
- General education assignment

LEVELS OF PROMPTING

Educators use many different prompting hierarchies. Most hierarchies follow the principle of least supportive levels of prompting to most supportive levels of prompting. Typically, the practice is to gradually move from more-supportive prompts to less-supportive prompts, fading them altogether whenever possible.

Discuss that a *prompt* is something that reminds or encourages someone to complete a task. Provide an example, such as verbally explaining the steps of a task or simply pointing at something to give a hint of what should be done next. Share that while prompts can be essential, they should only be used when needed. Emphasize that a student should always be given the opportunity to complete the task without any prompts. If they need prompts, always begin with the least intrusive, least supportive prompts, such as a gestural or modeling prompt, before moving on to more-supportive prompts. Only use more-supportive prompts, such as physical prompts, when absolutely necessary.

Discuss the downfall of peer tutors becoming habitual prompters. Tell them to avoid giving prompts before first determining how much prompting, if any, is needed. When prompts are automatically given, students may not have the opportunity to complete things they can do on their own.

After they have determined the appropriate level of prompting to use, remind peer tutors to consider fading to less-supportive prompts as soon as possible to allow the student to complete the task with less support and more independence. When explaining the different levels of prompting to students, use a very basic prompting hierarchy.

Have them role-play with a partner what different prompts look and sound like. Use figure 5.1 to discuss and practice with the whole group what each prompt looks and sounds like before pairing students to practice.

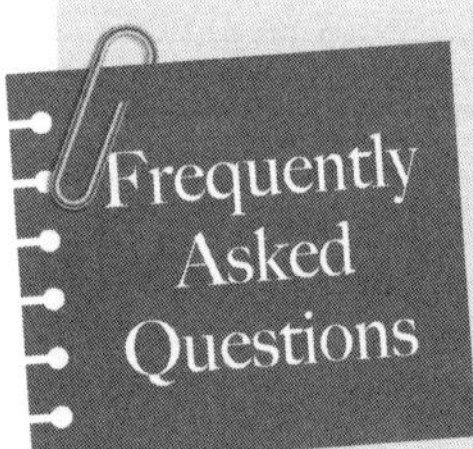

Is the prompting hierarchy the same as a multitiered system of supports (MTSS) and response to intervention (RTI)?

While related, a prompting hierarchy is actually a powerful tool used within MTSS and RTI, where educators increase tiered interventions based on the student's needs and fade them over time, with the shared goals of student independence and academic success.

What happens if a peer tutor fades a prompt too soon?

This is not a problem. Teach and guide peer tutors to reintroduce a previously faded prompt if a student shows signs of requiring more support to be successful.

Prompt	Looks Like . . .	Sounds Like . . .
Gestural Prompt Using a gesture to prompt a student on what they should do next	Shaking or nodding head Pointing at something	No sounds
Modeling Prompt Demonstrating exactly what you want the student to do so they can see what it is you are asking of them	Writing a complete sentence Filling in the blanks of a handout Measuring liquid into a beaker in a science lab	"Begin with a capital letter and end with a period, like this." [Models writing a complete sentence.] "I'll show you. You put a word on the line, just like this." [Models filling in the blanks.] "Pick up the beaker and pour the liquid until you reach the line, like this." [Models measuring liquid into a beaker.]
Visual Prompt Giving the student visual prompts, such as written words or pictures	Writing down the instructions for the student Showing the student a picture, graph, or table	"Read these instructions." "Look at this graph; it will help you understand what the teacher is saying and how you should complete the task."
Verbal Prompt Telling the student what to do or hinting at what you want them to do next	Facing the student Making eye contact Wearing a supportive expression	"First, open the book and find chapter 1." "Try looking at the bottom of the page; see if you can find it there."
Physical Prompt Guiding the student with a light physical touch to perform a task without doing it for them	Guiding an elbow to have the student reach for a pencil Placing your hand gently on top of theirs to guide their hand as they pour water into the beaker	"Is it okay if I help you pick up your pencil?" "If it is okay with you, I will guide your hand as you pour the water into the beaker."

Figure 5.1: *Example prompts.*

*Visit **go.SolutionTree.com/specialneeds** for a free reproducible version of this figure.*

CURRICULUM ACCESSIBILITY

Much of what peer tutors have learned thus far about support has been how to interact with students and how to teach and prompt them. This section pertains to the actual materials—the curricula—that students with disabilities receive and the ways it can be adapted to ensure accessibility. *Curricular adaptations*, indicating a change to the curriculum, is an umbrella term for both accommodations and modifications.

Explain to students the difference between accommodations and modifications; then, provide them with examples of each. Explain that *accommodations* are changes made that do not alter what the standards of the assignment or assessment are. Rather, they are changes in *how* students access the curriculum, *how* they are taught, or *how* they are assessed; the content level and performance criteria are not changed. Then, explain that *modifications* are changes to *what* the students are to learn and demonstrate, and they may alter the standards of the assignment. While there can be overlap between the two, table 5.1 provides simple examples.

Table 5.1: *Accommodation and Modification Examples*

Accommodations	Modifications
A teacher extending time for a student to complete a classroom writing assessment	A student writing a few sentences instead of an essay for the classroom assessment
A teacher enlarging the print of a mathematics activity sheet and spacing the problems out across the page to allow more white space for a student	A student completing an activity with multiplication facts for 0–2 instead of 0–12

Show students a wide variety of adaptations, ranging from simple accommodations to extensive modifications, and include both assignments and classroom assessments. Ask students to share any personal experiences with accommodations or modifications they have used either for themselves or for the student they are supporting.

Continue the discussion by reviewing the "Teaching Strategies and Accommodations" handout (page 111). Ask students which strategies they have already used and which new strategies might be beneficial. Next, have students get into small groups, and assign each group one of the scenarios from the "Student Case Studies for Curriculum Accessibility" activity (page 114). Provide them with a general education assignment of your choice and have them discuss teaching strategies and possible adaptations in small groups, based on their student case study. Once they have generated a list of suggestions, have them share their ideas with the whole class. Inquire as to which level of prompting students might try and what that would look like based on the case study.

Will peer tutors adapt curricula once they have completed this session?

No. The responsibility of designing curricular adaptations still lies with the general education teacher and the special education teacher. It is the peer tutor's role to implement any accommodations or modifications, such as reading text aloud or highlighting key words, under the direction of an educator. As the peer tutor gains more insight into what helps the student be more successful, they can contribute ideas for adaptations that will support the student with the curriculum. Many peer tutors realize that they are very skilled at finding meaningful ways to adapt curricula and, consequently, determine that a career in education is in their future. However, they should not implement these ideas without teacher approval and supervision.

Who is responsible for informing the peer tutor of any adaptations they should provide?

Both general and special educators are responsible for ensuring that students with disabilities receive any accommodations and modifications on their IEPs. Therefore, either educator—or both educators—can provide direction to a peer tutor in this regard.

HOMEWORK

Assign the next portion of the reproducible "Digital Portfolio Project" (page 99), Support Strategies and Curriculum Accessibility, for homework. The prompt listed on students' handout for the session two training is as follows.

> *Following this training, please ask the classroom teacher for an unadapted assignment from the class you provide support in. Considering any forms of support the student has been receiving and the things you have learned in this training, what teaching strategies, along with any adaptations to increase accessibility, would you suggest? Upload photographs or actual documents of the assignment and write a short paragraph explaining the steps required to make the assignment more accessible for your tutee. In addition, complete the "Levels of Prompting" handout and upload it to your portfolio.*

SUMMARY

This session provided peer tutors with valuable information on how to support students in general education classes. Peer tutors learned about five general prompting methods: (1) gestural, (2) modeling, (3) visual, (4) verbal, and (5) physical. More importantly, they learned about the potential risks of habitual prompting, which is a common tendency for peer tutors and educators when they first begin working with a student.

Peer tutors also learned what curricular adaptations are and how peer tutors can be part of a collaborative team that helps provide access to general education curricula for the students they support. Learning about teaching strategies and curricular adaptations strengthens peer tutors' knowledge and skills, ultimately promoting more successful inclusion for all students.

TEACHING STRATEGIES AND ACCOMMODATIONS

Not all of these strategies will apply to every student you support. Tailor accommodations and modifications to the specific assignment, as well as the individual strengths and needs of the student you are supporting. **Always communicate with educators prior to implementing a new strategy or accommodation.** The following table provides ideas and examples.

Strategy or Accommodation	Example
Break down information into small steps and simplify instructions.	Instead of saying, "Finish this worksheet and turn it in," say the following. "Write your name at the top of the page." "Write an answer for questions one through five." "Take the worksheet to your teacher when you are finished."
Decrease the amount of material the student is expected to learn or complete.	Instead of having the student learn how to read all twenty words, have them learn how to read five words, and then move on.
Provide the student with answers to choose from, rather than asking open-ended questions.	Instead of asking, "How many eyes did the cyclops have?," ask, "Did the cyclops have *one* eye or *three* eyes?"
Repeat instructions. After repeating twice, say the instructions using different vocabulary or give an example of what you are explaining or asking.	1. State the request: "Please put your sketchbook in your backpack." 2. Wait ten seconds. 3. Repeat the request: "Please put your sketchbook in your backpack." 4. Wait ten seconds. 5. Rephrase the request. For example, you could say, "Take your sketchbook off your desk and put it inside the bag where you put your stuff."
Always provide the student with the least amount of help necessary, allowing them to do as much on their own as possible.	In a science lab, allow the student to collect all the needed materials independently, and observe the student as they pour the liquid into the beaker. If the student is pouring too fast, verbally prompt them to slow down, or model it for them.

Strategy or Accommodation	Example
Show the student how to do a task by modeling it or providing an example.	In an art class, imagine that students are asked to cut out strips of colored paper. Prior to the student beginning this task, cut out one strip to demonstrate where the student should cut. Show an example of the correct-sized strip to the student if needed.
Give real-life examples when explaining difficult concepts.	When the class is learning about the concept of foreshadowing, have the student think about how dark rain clouds predict (foreshadow) rain.
Provide encouragement and positive comments.	Say something encouraging; for example, "I like how descriptive your sentences are."
Allow time for the student to process their thoughts.	Avoid repeating prompts or questions if the student needs more time to process what was said to them.
Create sentences with blanks that the student can fill in.	Give the student the opportunity to fill in missing words in a sentence (for example, "The main character has a conflict with ________").
Use graph paper to line up numbers for mathematics problems.	Write numbers within the boxes of graph paper to make it clear which column of numbers to add or subtract.
Consider using more visuals (such as pictures), **written instructions**, or a **concept map**.	For example, when students are learning about the word *cell* in science class, show the student a picture of a cell to accompany the written word.
Encourage the student to visualize what they are reading.	After the student reads a short passage about people on an island, have them close their eyes and imagine the sounds and sites of the waves on the beach.

Strategy or Accommodation	Example
Provide verbal prompting as needed to complete tasks.	Verbally prompt the student to finish a task. For example, you might say, "It's time to put your lab materials in the yellow bins" or indirectly prompt, "What do you need to do now?"
Use a color-coding system to help the student keep a notebook organized.	Communicate where assignments go. For example, you might say, "Put all of your math homework in the purple folder; then, put all of your history homework in the blue folder."
Underline or highlight important words.	Ask the student if they prefer key words to be underlined or highlighted.
Use flashcards to study key points and vocabulary words.	Using blank note cards, assist the student in creating their own flashcards for studying class content.
Assist student with note taking.	If the student is not able to take notes independently, share the responsibility by writing down essential information while encouraging the student to record as much as they can.
Read materials aloud.	If the student is expected to read materials that are difficult for them, quietly read the materials aloud, explaining the content as necessary.
Assist the student with using a computer when completing written work.	If a student needs help navigating computer programs or applications to complete an assignment, provide guidance by pointing to the screen to show where the student should click or type.
Write down answers if the student is dictating responses.	If a student knows the answers but has difficulty writing them down, record their verbal responses and note that the student dictated the responses.

STUDENT CASE STUDIES FOR CURRICULUM ACCESSIBILITY

This handout has case studies that you can cut out and provide to students in small groups. Each group should receive one case study and one assignment of your choice. Have the groups discuss teaching strategies and possible adaptations, based on their designated student case study. After they list suggestions, they share with the whole group and answer the following questions.

Which level of prompting might you try?

What would that look like based on your case study?

Mia

Mia is an eleventh grader who loves going to musicals. She uses a power wheelchair. She is unable to grasp a writing utensil, so she uses a keyboard to write. She reads at the first-grade level and writes simple sentences. She enjoys using the internet to conduct research and find answers for her homework assignments. She benefits from listening to audiobooks. She is learning how to add single-digit numbers. While she is able to say several words, she uses a voice output device to communicate many of her thoughts.

Reina

Reina is an eleventh grader who loves to talk about television shows. While she cannot read Spanish, she fluently speaks it. She is learning to read and write simple words in English. She can add and subtract single-digit numbers. She is a diligent worker and works best when someone is there to help her stay focused on the task at hand. She often needs to be given an example of what she is being asked to complete.

Roscoe

Roscoe is a tenth grader and is an amazing dancer and singer. He reads at the third-grade level. He is able to write a five-sentence paragraph. He responds best to comprehension questions when he is given only two choices. He often has difficulty understanding steps in a task. Having someone explain the directions and give him examples helps tremendously. He can add and subtract two-digit numbers and is learning division.

Ava

Ava is a tenth grader who loves the color purple. She communicates using picture communication cards (cards with pictures that represent what she wants or how she feels). She often needs reminders to use her cards. She can say some words and speaks very softly. She can trace dotted letters. She comprehends material when it is accompanied by pictures. She can identify numbers 1 through 10.

Reym

Reym is a twelfth grader who collects baseball cards. He reads at the fourth-grade level. He needs help with understanding assignment directions. He is often unsure of himself, so he needs encouragement to continue working on an assignment. When he doesn't understand something, he stops working and doesn't ask for help. When asked what is wrong, he will often state that it is too hard. However, when given examples of what he should be doing, he can be very successful. He prefers to complete his assignments on the computer rather than by hand, as his writing is not very legible, and he needs help with spelling. He is learning multiplication facts.

Levi

Levi is a ninth grader who loves to talk about movie facts. He prefers to follow a routine and needs to be informed ahead of time about any changes to his daily schedule. Noises can be distracting to him. He follows directions best when they are written down for him rather than spoken to him. He needs a five-minute break about every ten or fifteen minutes. This break can include writing in his journal or going to the restroom or drinking fountain. He reads at the sixth-grade level and is a skilled writer. He understands what he reads very well but needs plenty of time to process what is being asked of him. He is learning how to complete basic algebraic equations.

LEVELS OF PROMPTING

Name: ______________________________________ Date: ________________

Give examples for each of the prompt types in the following table. If possible, include examples of prompts you have actually used with a student.

Prompt	**Example**
Gestural prompt	
Modeling prompt	
Visual prompt	
Verbal prompt	
Physical prompt	

CHAPTER 6

Session Three: Communication

Interacting with others, making choices, and expressing feelings are critical skills for students to learn. In addition, teaching communication to students with extensive support needs is essential for learning, as what they learn is often dependent on their interactions with others (Pinto, Simpson, & Bakken, 2009).

I learned more about geography because I was a peer tutor. I learned just as much as any other student enrolled in the class.

—Peer tutor

Session three is designed to inform peer tutors about how important communication is for everyone, how important it is that students are taught and given tools to communicate effectively, and what the peer tutors' role is in supporting these skills.

The student learning objective for session three: Students will learn the importance of effective communication skills and will be better prepared to facilitate communication among students.

You will need the following materials.

- Index cards with your own messages or the messages provided in this chapter

For the communication cards, consider making each A-B pair on separate index cards of the same color. For example, put the A *I'm hungry* card and the B *I'm hungry* card on yellow index cards, the A *I'm sad* card and the B *I'm sad* card on blue index cards, and so on.

DEFINITIONS OF *COMMUNICATION*, *LANGUAGE*, AND *SPEECH*

Before moving on to any subsequent activities in this session, peer tutors must first develop a clear understanding of what is required for communication to occur, what constitutes language, and how speech is only one of many ways to communicate.

Begin the lesson by having students brainstorm possible definitions for the terms *communication*, *language*, and *speech*. A simple and practical definition for *communication* is "information transferred from one to another." To help students arrive at this definition, provide them with examples of the following.

- Information *successfully* transferred from one person to another, such as chatting with friends back and forth via text messages
- Information *unsuccessfully* transferred from one person to another, such as talking to someone who is ultrafocused on their phone

Make the point that for communication to occur, information has to actually be transferred from one person to another. Students will come up with several definitions of the term *language*, and all may be correct. *Language* is an arbitrary set of symbols (words) agreed on by the users as a means to communicate. These arbitrary symbols take on meaning when they are agreed on by most of those who use the language.

One point to make is that new vocabulary is developing all the time. You may want to invite the students to share examples of newer words or phrases currently trending among teenagers. This can be a fun way for students to understand that new vocabulary is forming all the time, and words are only meaningful when others agree on their meanings.

Explain that *speech* is simply the oral method of representing language. Discuss how speech is not the only method of communication and ask students to provide examples of other ways to communicate, such as:

- Sign language
- Body language
- Facial expressions
- Verbal expressions that are not words
- Picture pointing
- Augmentative and alternative communication devices
- Eye gazing

Following this discussion, peer tutors should have a basic understanding of the meanings of *communication*, *language*, and *speech*. They are now ready to take language apart even further by looking at the differences between receptive language and expressive language.

RECEPTIVE VERSUS EXPRESSIVE LANGUAGE

There are two essential components of communication: (1) receptive communication and (2) expressive communication. *Receptive communication* is the input side of language. It involves receiving, processing, and understanding messages from others. This side of communication allows us to understand and interpret what we see and hear.

Expressive communication is the output side of language. It allows us to convey feelings, needs, wants, likes, dislikes, and ideas. And as we noted earlier, expressive communication can occur in many ways, such as speech and other vocalizations, sign language, body language, gestures, speech output devices, and so on.

Begin a discussion by asking peer tutors to share what they think the terms *receptive communication* and *expressive communication* mean. As the discussion develops, help tutors arrive at similar definitions (as given earlier in this section), and ask them to consider what each type of communication might look like when interacting with students. It may be helpful to pair the *receptive communication* definition with a context in which peer tutors might experience it with students. For example, letting them know that if a student follows directions or responds to a greeting or question in a way that makes sense, one can assume that receptive communication has occurred.

Ask peer tutors to share, without using names, a time when they observed someone expressing themselves in a different way, and whether they understood what the person conveyed to them.

The corresponding What am I trying to say? activity involves both parts of communication. It is a fun way for students to arrive at the overarching ideas that teaching communication skills is essential and that being part of a collaborative team—like theirs—can help support the development of these very important skills.

For this activity, have students get into pairs. Give each student in the pair a message to communicate, one labeled *A* and one labeled *B*.

- The A message should be very simple.
- The B message should be a much more complex version of the simple statement in message A.

You can use the messages provided in figure 6.1 or create your own.

A Messages	B Messages
I'm hungry.	I hope we are having chili cheese dogs today because I'm tired of hot dogs with ketchup and mustard.
I'm thirsty.	I need to drink more water, but I would rather have a cherry-flavored slushy.
I'm tired.	I am really tired, but I hope I can stay awake until 11:30 p.m. so I can finish watching my movie.
I'm sad.	I am sad that I haven't seen my mom in three weeks, and I hope someone can help me call her.
I want to go for a ride.	I want someone to take me to the mall so I can buy my favorite perfume, which is made by CHANEL.

Figure 6.1: *Sample messages for the What am I trying to say? activity.*
Visit ***go.SolutionTree.com/specialneeds*** *for a free reproducible version of this figure.*

Tell students that they will need to communicate the messages to each other without speaking or writing. Begin by having students with the A card communicate their message. Students should be able to complete this portion of the activity relatively quickly and effortlessly. Then, have students holding the B card communicate their message to their partner. Students will have a very difficult time communicating B messages.

After all students have had time to attempt to express their messages, ask them to share with the class what their messages were. Hold a discussion regarding the differences between the A messages and the B messages. Talk about how it felt to try to get their partner to understand what they were trying to communicate.

Make the following points in your discussion.

- **A person's thoughts may be more complex than they initially seem.** Many students are capable of having complex thoughts but are unable to communicate them.
- **A person may feel frustrated when they are unable to communicate their thoughts fully.** This, unfortunately, can result in people resorting to unconventional ways to communicate their needs, including challenging behaviors like vocal outbursts or acts of physical aggression. If this is the case with any students that peer tutors are working with or around, take care to explain in a respectful manner (not singling out one particular student) that these behaviors are often attempts to communicate unmet needs or frustration from not being understood.

- **A person may stop communicating altogether after unsuccessful attempts.** When students are not taught how to communicate effectively, whether due to a lack of support, tools, or instruction, they may eventually develop the belief that others will never understand them and stop trying to communicate at all (Downing, Hanreddy, & Peckham-Hardin, 2015).

It is incredibly important that peer tutors be aware of these possible consequences and let teachers know as soon as possible if they are experiencing any communication issues. The special education teacher or the student's speech-language pathologist can provide the peer tutor with possible learning and communication strategies specific to that student, as well as prompts that could be helpful to them, such as visual communication tools.

INSIGHTS FROM A SPEECH-LANGUAGE PATHOLOGIST

Speech-language pathologists play a critical role in supporting peer tutors with the communication needs of students. They receive extensive training and are experts in how people communicate and how to help when communication difficulties arise. They are trained to work with varying degrees of communication needs, ranging from teaching pragmatics (what to say, how to say it, and when to say it in social situations) to teaching students to use speech-generating devices. Introduce SLPs to peer tutors as soon as possible and explain that they are a valuable resource for successful inclusion and peer tutor experiences.

After completing the What am I trying to say? activity, invite an SLP to discuss general strategies used with students who need support communicating. If there is time, they can meet briefly with each of the peer tutors at this session to provide strategies that are specific to the student they are working with. If time does not allow for this, the SLP can schedule brief meetings at a later date to discuss strategies with each peer tutor.

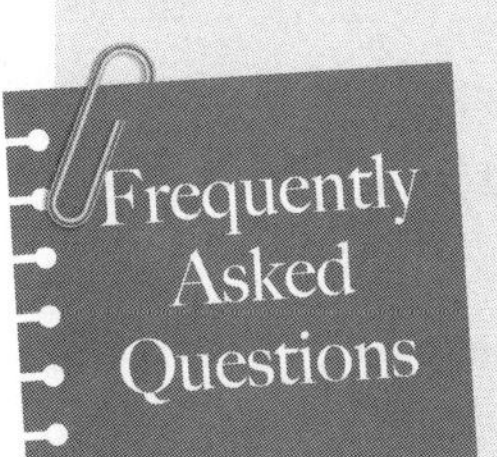

Where should speech-language pathologists work with peer tutors who are supporting students in general education classes?

There is much to be said for providing instruction in the environments where the support for communication is needed. If possible, SLPs should work with peer tutors in the general education classrooms where the tutors are supporting students. This allows for collaboration among the SLP and peer tutor, as well as the general education teacher. However, if this collaboration would disrupt the general education setting, set up appointments in the SLP's or special educator's office instead.

Will general education teachers be familiar with all the services that SLPs provide?

Yes. The general education teacher should be aware of all the services that the SLP will provide to any student in their class. This information is on a student's IEP, which all of their teachers can access. In addition, many special educators provide general educators with an abbreviated version of an IEP—often referred to as an *IEP at a Glance* or a *Student Snapshot*—that teachers can quickly and easily reference.

HOMEWORK

Assign the next portion of the reproducible "Digital Portfolio Project" (page 99), Communication, for homework. The prompt listed on students' handout for session three training is as follows.

> *Following this training, please write two paragraphs about communication. One paragraph should explain the importance of teaching communication skills to students. The second paragraph should explain specific strategies you could use to help the student you work with learn better communication skills. Add two additional photographs to your portfolio that capture people communicating and how communication relates to your role as a peer tutor. Examples of photographs to use could include students using communication devices, interacting in cooperative group learning activities, or participating in class presentations.*

SUMMARY

This session helped peer tutors discover how important it is to help students develop effective communication skills. Tutors learned what the parts to communication are (receptive and expressive language) and experienced how it feels when other people are unable to understand what they are trying to communicate. Not being understood has some negative consequences, such as people perceiving that a student is incapable of having complex thoughts, students experiencing frustration from struggling to communicate, and students ultimately giving up on communication. While scary, these consequences are less likely to occur when students are taught communication skills in an effective manner, one that involves a collaborative approach between educators and SLPs. With support and training from professionals, peer tutors can be part of this collaborative effort.

CHAPTER 7

Session Four: Social Inclusion

For many students, high school becomes much more than going to classes, getting good grades, and experiencing academic growth. During this time, students develop friendships and shared interests, and they often remember the social aspect of high school most, not the curriculum. High school can be a place where students feel supported and included. However, for some, it can be a place of loneliness or stress, depending on their experiences (Rahman, 2025).

I feel being a tutor for an English class helped me a lot. Now that I have [that] English [class] myself, I feel more confident about the work I do.

—Peer tutor

Because students with disabilities may experience additional barriers to forming friendships, such as lacking communication skills or having different social behaviors, they are in danger of experiencing loneliness. It is for this reason that this session trains peer tutors how to help facilitate social interactions for the students they are paired with.

The student learning objective for session four: Students will learn the importance of friendships and social interactions for all students and will be better prepared to facilitate social interactions.

You will need the following materials.

- Projector or chart paper
- Reproducible "Circle of Friends" (page 132)
- Reproducible "Perception Scripts" (page 133)

- Reproducible "Strategies for Facilitating Social Interactions—Example Student Amari" (page 134)
- Reproducible "Strategies for Facilitating Social Interactions" (page 135)
- Reproducible "Scenarios for Student Involvement" (page 136)
- Access to a video of your choice

FRIENDSHIP QUOTE INTERPRETATION

Begin your lesson by showing the following translation of a quote from Aristotle (ca. 340 B.C.E./1886) on a screen or on chart paper: "[Friendship] is a sort of virtue, or at least implies virtue, and is, moreover, most necessary to our life. For no one would care to live without friends, though he had all other good things" (p. 251). Ask students to take a few minutes to discuss this quote with the person sitting next to them. Have them reflect on whether they agree or disagree with the statement. Ask for volunteers to share what they discussed.

FRIENDSHIP QUALITIES AND CIRCLE OF FRIENDS

After students have agreed on the importance of friendship, the discussion can move to what it is that they value in a friend and what their friend groups currently look like. Begin with the following questions, encouraging responses from as many peer tutors as possible.

- "What makes a good friend?"
- "What do you like to do with your friends?"
- "What are some of the things you talk about with your friends?"

Once students have answered all three questions and shared their values, have each student complete the reproducible "Circle of Friends" (page 132). Discuss each circle one at a time and ask volunteers to share who they put in each circle. Educators can share who they put in theirs as well. Discuss that while everyone's circles may be a little different, the hope is that everyone is given opportunities in all of these circles to meet and interact with others. Share how some people might have circles that are empty or not as full, and ask what might cause this. It could be that some students may not have the necessary support to engage in as many social activities as others.

Then, begin a discussion about the importance of facilitating opportunities within these circles where friendships might naturally develop. For students with smaller inner circles, facilitating classroom interactions may be beneficial, as these interactions can expand their social networks and create opportunities for friendship. Some students may need support with the social skills necessary to start conversations or engage in activities. Have students brainstorm the social skills and communication skills needed when interacting with others.

Having the communication skills necessary for social interactions involves understanding the rules of communication, which include initiating a greeting, taking turns, and asking open-ended questions. For some students, being able to use augmentative and alternative communication devices to interact with others is another necessary communication skill. It is also important to encourage students to be aware of which students in the classroom share similar interests and to learn how to strike up a conversation.

It's important for everyone to have the opportunities and social skills to fill up their circles if they choose. These activities and discussions prepare students for the strategies covered in the next section.

FACILITATION OF SOCIAL INTERACTIONS

The activities and discussions from this session so far have led peer tutors to the understanding that friendships are important and that social interactions don't come easily for everyone. You can now provide them with some specific strategies for facilitating social interactions for the students they work with.

However, before doing so, it is important for teachers to know and share with peer tutors that this training is not suggesting that they must become friends with the students they support. Rather, it is encouraging them to facilitate social interactions for the students they support so that there is space for natural friendships to develop. Despite this clarification, natural friendships sometimes form between peer tutors and the students they support, and educators should encourage that friendship.

After making clear what the training's focus is, begin a discussion about the following general strategies.

- **Opportunities:** Have students brainstorm ways they can provide opportunities for students to have more social interactions. Examples could include encouraging students to say "hi" to people they know or introducing them to other students. While in class, the peer tutor could make sure that the student they support is in proximity to other students, and they could encourage the student to get involved in class or group activities.

- **Accommodations:** Discuss the importance of always considering what a person needs to be able to participate in an activity. For example, if students are playing baseball, we could allow a student who uses a wheelchair to be pushed around the bases by a teammate. If students are preparing group presentations, consider the skills the student needs in order to contribute and any accommodations that can ensure they are included.
- **Perceptions:** Discuss the importance of using intentional words when talking about others, specifically students with disabilities. Our language should highlight students in ways that reflect their strengths and positive qualities. A clever way to illustrate how important word choice is and how it affects others' perceptions is to have students role-play two scenarios about a student. Cut out the cards from the reproducible "Perception Scripts" (page 133). Script 1 describes a student negatively, while script 2 describes them positively. Have two students read the first (negative) script. Ask them to tell how speaker 1 is likely to respond to the last question, based on the exchange they just had. Then, have two other students read the second (positive) script, and again, ask how speaker 1 is likely to respond to the last question. Then, point out to the students that the two descriptions are of the same person. This type of skit makes clear that the way they talk about other students really does make a difference.

Next, pass out the reproducible "Strategies for Facilitating Social Interactions—Example Student Amari" (page 134). Some of these strategies overlap with the three general strategies we discussed earlier, yet they provide more detail. Go over each of the strategies listed and challenge the students to come up with ideas that are specific to the student they are working with. Use the blank reproducible "Strategies for Facilitating Social Interactions" (page 135).

Do peer tutors ever develop friendships with their assigned tutee?

Absolutely! As mentioned, it is not required, but sometimes these friendships form quite naturally and even lead to an increase in social opportunities outside of the school day. Peer tutors may believe that they can't socialize with their tutee outside of their peer tutor role. Special educators can help facilitate this if they see natural friendships developing.

FACILITATION OF STUDENT INVOLVEMENT IN GROUP ACTIVITIES

Have students get into small groups, and provide them with the reproducible "Scenarios for Student Involvement" (page 136). Assign each group to one scenario, which includes a description of a student and a group assignment from that student's class. Ask each group to take about five or ten minutes to determine how its student can best participate in the activity. While students work in groups, do a brief check-in with them and offer suggestions as needed. Then, have each group share its case studies and suggestions with the whole class.

After each group presents its scenarios to the class, teachers should acknowledge and compliment all suggestions and ask the whole group if anyone thought of additional suggestions for this particular scenario. By the time all scenarios have been discussed, peer tutors should have a better sense of how to include students in classroom activities.

FRIENDSHIP VIDEOS

Short videos showing stories of friendship among students with and without disabilities can be a perfect way to wrap up this session. We recommend playing videos that highlight the importance of friendships, as well as debriefing scripts, reflection questions, and purposes for each. Show one of these two videos (or seek others that better reflect the needs of your school community).

Land of 10,000 Stories: 2nd Grade Friendship Binds HS Honor Student, Teen With Autism (KARE 11, 2018) provides a better understanding of how long-term kindness and empathy can impact friendships and foster meaningful inclusion in schools. You can try this script for setting the tone.

> *As we talked about earlier in this training session, people experience friendships and disability in different ways. When discussing this video, please talk respectfully and listen carefully to others' thoughts and opinions.*

You can pose the following questions.

- "What did you like or notice about the friendship shown in this video?"
- "What did you think about how Tre treated Adam?"
- "How do you think this friendship felt for both Tre and Adam?"
- "Tre was there for Adam at times when he needed him. Think about a time when a friend was there for you. How did it make you feel, and why are friendships so important?"

- "Without mentioning any names, do you see any friendships at our school like the one Tre and Adam have?"
- "Can you think of ways that we can be good friends to people who are different from us?"

You can close with something like the following.

This video shows that friendship is about being there for one another, treating each other with respect, and showing care over time. Our differences don't have to get in the way. Each of us can help others feel seen, valued, and included.

Another possibility is *Voices of Friendship (1996)*, a video by the University of New Hampshire Institute on Disability (2011). This video helps students think about friendship, inclusion, empathy, and the power of words and actions. You can try the following script for setting the tone.

As we talked about earlier in this training session, people experience friendship and disability in different ways. When discussing this video, please talk respectfully and listen carefully to others' thoughts and opinions.

You can pose the following questions.

- "What kinds of challenges did the students experience in their friendship?"
- "Did anyone's voice or story in the video stand out to you?"
- "When Jocelyn's friend said, 'I've learned so much with Jocelyn than I've learned in my ten years of school,' what do you think she meant?"
- "Without mentioning any names, do you see situations like this happening on our campus?"
- "Did you get any ideas from this video about how you could facilitate friendships for others?"

You can close with something like the script shared for the preceding video.

HOMEWORK

Assign the next portion of the "Digital Portfolio Project" (page 99), Social Inclusion, for homework. The prompt listed on students' handout for session four training is as follows.

Following this training, please complete the handout "Strategies for Facilitating Social Interactions." Provide examples of strategies you could use to increase social interactions for the student you are working with. An example of how to complete this assignment is given in the handout "Strategies for Facilitating Social Interactions—Example Student Amari." Add two additional photographs to your portfolio that capture what facilitating social interactions looks like and how it relates to your role as a peer tutor. Examples of photographs to use include social activities and interactions, both in and out of the classroom.

SUMMARY

This session was full of activities and discussions that guided peer tutors in understanding the importance of friendships. They examined their own friendships and recognized that social interactions do not come easily to everyone. By learning different strategies to encourage social interactions, peer tutors gained the knowledge and confidence to play an important role in creating social opportunities for the students they support.

CIRCLE OF FRIENDS

Follow these steps.

1. Put your name in the center circle.
2. In the second circle, put the names of people in your life who are closest to you: family members, romantic partner, best friend, and so on.
3. In the third circle, write the names of your good friends and people you spend time with often.
4. In the fourth circle, write the names of people (or group of people) you know through organizations, clubs, sports teams, or community groups you are involved with.
5. In the outermost circle, write the names of people who are paid to provide services to you: teachers, doctors, counselors, and other professionals.

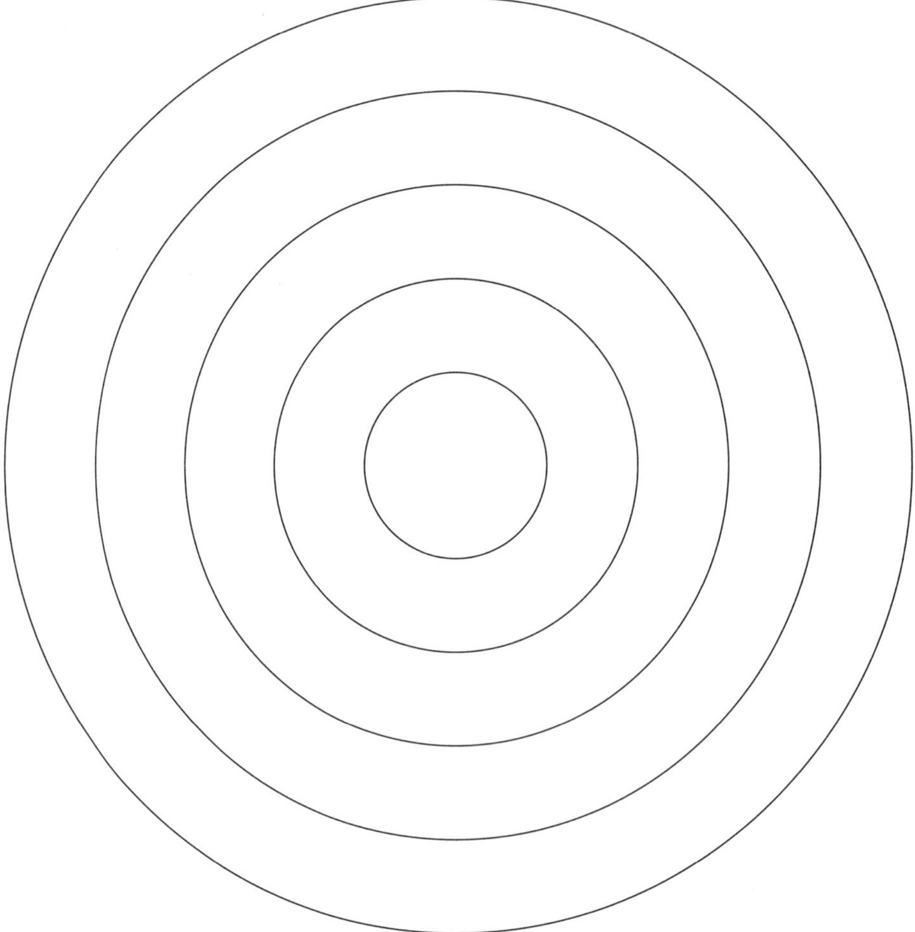

Source: Adapted with permission. Copyright 1994 by Marsha Forest, Judith Snow, and Jack Pearpoint. From Hints for Graphic Facilitators *by Jack Pearpoint. Published by Inclusion Press, 47 Indian Trail, Toronto, ON M6R 1Z8, inclusion.com.*

PERCEPTION SCRIPTS

Cut out individual scripts to use in a role-playing activity.

SCRIPT 1

Speaker 1: Hey, what are you doing tonight?

Speaker 2: I have to go to the game with this guy from my English class. Do you want to go with us?

Speaker 1: I don't know. Tell me about this guy.

Speaker 2: Well, he always asks a lot of questions and always wants to stand too close to other people. Sometimes he even touches my hair. He is so distracted that he doesn't even notice when he bumps into you. Anyway, do you want to go with us?

Speaker 1: ______________________________

____

____

SCRIPT 1

Speaker 1: Hey, what are you doing tonight?

Speaker 2: I have to go to the game with this guy from my English class. Do you want to go with us?

Speaker 1: I don't know. Tell me about this guy.

Speaker 2: Well, he always asks a lot of questions and always wants to stand too close to other people. Sometimes he even touches my hair. He is so distracted that he doesn't even notice when he bumps into you. Anyway, do you want to go with us?

Speaker 1: ______________________________

____

____

SCRIPT 2

Speaker 1: Hey, what are you doing tonight?

Speaker 2: I'm going to the game with this guy from my English class. Do you want to go with us?

Speaker 1: I don't know. Tell me about this guy.

Speaker 2: Well, he is super friendly and always wants to know all about you. He is on the track team and loves football. He is always making me laugh. Anyway, do you want to go with us?

Speaker 1: ______________________________

____

____

SCRIPT 2

Speaker 1: Hey, what are you doing tonight?

Speaker 2: I'm going to the game with this guy from my English class. Do you want to go with us?

Speaker 1: I don't know. Tell me about this guy.

Speaker 2: Well, he is super friendly and always wants to know all about you. He is on the track team and loves football. He is always making me laugh. Anyway, do you want to go with us?

Speaker 1: ______________________________

____

____

STRATEGIES FOR FACILITATING SOCIAL INTERACTIONS—EXAMPLE STUDENT AMARI

The following table provides examples of ways you can use strategies to foster social interactions, using an imaginary student named Amari.

Strategy	Example
Model ways for other students to interact.	"Amari would be able to sing this song if you shared the printed lyrics with him."
Make sure your student is sitting near other students.	"Amari, why don't you go sit with your lab group?"
Ask peers to help your student with specific tasks.	"Mary, will you help Amari with this worksheet?"
Redirect interactions from your student.	"Amari, please see if Jada will help you."
Positively interpret the student's behavior for others.	"That usually means that Amari is feeling nervous."
Redirect interactions to your student.	"Asking Amari himself is how I know how he is. I make sure he can see me when I ask."
Teach interaction skills to your student.	"Amari, let's practice asking a friend to meet you at lunch."
Highlight similarities among students.	"Wow, you both like country music!"

Source: Adapted from The Center on Secondary Education for Students with Autism Spectrum Disorder. (n.d.). Peer supports facilitator manual. *Author. Accessed at https://csesa.fpg.unc.edu/sites/csesa.fpg.unc.edu/files/Peer%20Supports%20Manual.pdf on October 7, 2025.*

STRATEGIES FOR FACILITATING SOCIAL INTERACTIONS

Record ideas that are specific to the student you are working with. Refer to "Strategies for Facilitating Social Interactions—Example Student Amari" if that is helpful.

Specific Ideas for Facilitating Social Interactions for

__________________________ in __________________________ class.

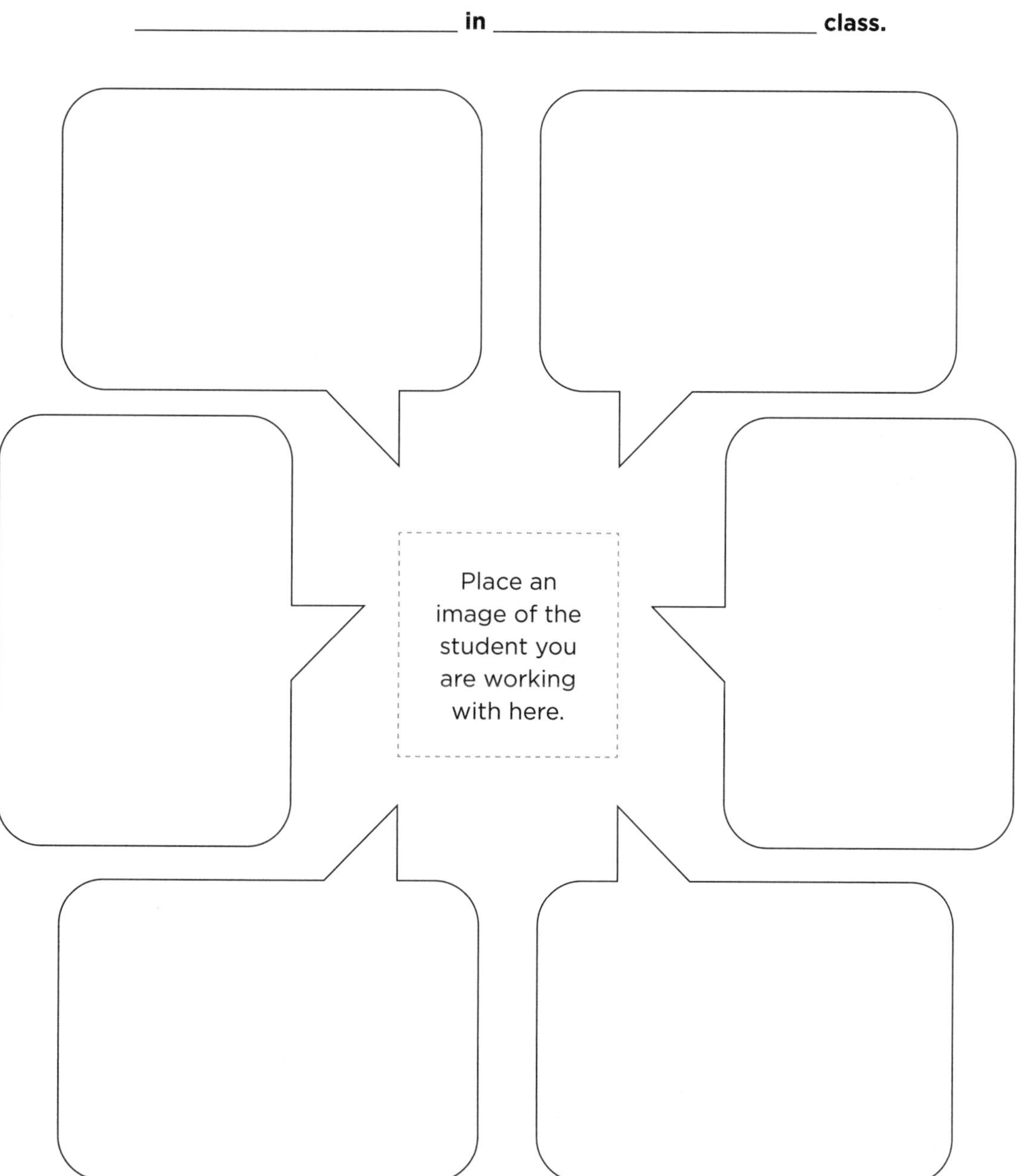

SCENARIOS FOR STUDENT INVOLVEMENT

As a group, read your assigned case study and class activity. In the given time, determine how your scenario student can best participate in the activity. You will share your case study and suggestions with the whole class.

Scenario 1

Matt is a tenth grader who loves people and has a great sense of humor. He can write his own name independently and trace letters and words. Matt can read some small words that he has memorized, but his comprehension is best when material is presented to him orally. He can read picture communication symbols and—with some support from his peer tutor—obtain pictures from the internet and magazines. Matt enjoys interacting with his classmates and especially loves presenting in front of the class.

Review the assignment from Matt's oceanography class and determine how he can best complete the assignment and be involved with his group.

Oceanography—Report on a Species

Your group has been asked to write a paper and create a poster about a species that lives in the ocean. Your group will need to research its chosen species and find pictures to put on the poster. Finally, your group will give a three-to-five-minute presentation of its findings to the class.

Scenario 2

Garrett is a ninth grader who loves music and enjoys other people interacting with him. He has no vision in either eye and does not speak. He is beginning to learn how to use a simple communication device that has twelve everyday messages on it, including "yes," "no," "hi," "bye," and so on. Garrett also has a communication device that can be programmed for special communication opportunities. For example, it can provide scripts for communicating with others or for participating in activities (like class plays). It is important for Garrett to have as many opportunities as possible to use his communication device.

Review the assignment from Garrett's English language arts class and determine how he can best complete the assignment and be involved with his group.

English Language Arts—Performance of Two Scenes From *Romeo and Juliet*

Your group has been assigned to act out two scenes from *Romeo and Juliet*. Each person must have a part in the play. The parts do not have to be memorized. After the play is complete, students will be required to answer twenty comprehension questions about it.

Scenario 3

Marc is an eleventh grader who loves to talk about sports. His speech is not easily understood by everyone, but as people get to know him, he becomes easier to understand. He uses gestures to help others understand him. Marc can copy words, but he prefers to type on a keyboard. He can read some small words but understands picture symbols better. Marc gets frustrated when he perceives his work to be less than perfect. This may cause him to stop working temporarily.

Review the assignment from Marc's history class and determine how he can best complete the assignment and be involved with his group.

History—Research Paper and Presentation on World War II

Your group has been asked to research World War II. The final project will include a paper summarizing the events of the war and a poster with pictures representing the events of the war. You will present your findings to the class in a three-to-five-minute presentation.

Scenario 4

Kaylynn is in the twelfth grade and loves to hang out with her girlfriends. She enjoys shopping and always knows about the latest fashions. She can read at about the third-grade level. She can write a paragraph and is working on improving her grammar and varying her sentence structure. Her speech is easy to understand, but she is a little nervous about speaking in front of a crowd.

Review the assignment from Kaylynn's American Government class and determine how she can best complete the assignment and be involved with her group.

American Government—Research Project on a Special Interest Group

Your group will research a special interest group of your choice. The final project will include a minimum of five pages detailing what the mission of your special interest group is, how this group accomplishes its goals, and how effective it is at doing so. Your job is to convince your readers why they should become involved with the mission of your group. In addition to the written product, your group will present its findings to the class and attempt to convince audience members that they should become a part of this movement.

Scenario 5

Brett is an eleventh grader who enjoys learning about wildlife. He uses a wheelchair and needs to be pushed wherever he goes. Brett loves to look at books with pictures, and he likes to listen to people read. He has limited use of his hands and arms. He can point to pictures but is rarely able to pick up items in a purposeful manner. Brett uses a joystick mouse on the computer and can select items and drag them to appropriate locations on the screen. Brett uses a voice output device to communicate simple messages. He is working on being able to combine words to create messages that are more like sentences.

Review the assignment from Brett's English language arts class and determine how he can best complete the assignment and be involved with his group.

English Language Arts—Greek Mythology Newspaper

Your group has been asked to create a newspaper. The theme of the paper is Greek mythology. There should be a variety of things in the paper: articles, pictures, ads, and comics. The newspaper should reflect Greek times.

CHAPTER 8
Session Five: Book Talk

Assigning a class book, particularly a fictional book that includes a character with a disability, can be an effective way for peer tutors to build knowledge and deepen their understanding of human differences. Benefits from reading fiction include enhanced empathy, social-cognitive abilities, and *theory of mind*, which is the ability to understand how other people think and feel (Mar, Oatley, Hirsh, dela Paz, & Peterson, 2006; Tamir, Bricker, Dodell-Feder, & Mitchell, 2015). Empathy and theory of mind are central to the goals of this peer tutoring course.

> *[Peer tutoring] helped prepare me and confirm my desire to become a special education teacher. It also made me want to reach out and volunteer with this community, or any people who need [support], in my spare time.*
>
> **—Peer tutor**

The student learning objective for session five: Students will gain insight into the perspectives of individuals with disabilities and their needs by reading a novel that portrays a character with a disability's point of view.

You will need the following materials.

- Access to a class set of a book (educator's choice)
- Discussion questions

BOOK TALK

This activity gives peer tutors opportunities to relate to characters with disabilities and, in doing so, gain a deeper understanding of others. When young people engage with a fictional world through reading and connect with characters, their empathy is enhanced (Bal & Veltkamp, 2013; Roza & Guimarães, 2022).

You can give this lesson anytime; however, we recommend assigning it midway through the course, as this activity spans the two to three weeks necessary for students to read their book. While there are many novels that do an exceptional job portraying characters with disabilities, two of our favorites are *Stuck in Neutral* by Terry Trueman (2000) and *Out of My Mind* by Sharon M. Draper (2010). We provide written activities for these two novels at the end of this chapter. (See the reproducibles "*Stuck in Neutral* by Terry Trueman," page 142, and "*Out of My Mind* by Sharon M. Draper," page 145.) You can also search online for premade activities to complement these two novels.

It is important to consider the following aspects when deciding which book to read.

- **The needs of the students currently supported by peer tutors:** Choosing a book that includes characters who share similar needs or experiences to students at their school can lead to powerful moments of understanding and more meaningful discussions. These conversations can foster empathy and help peer tutors recognize and reflect on assumptions they may not have realized they had.
- **The training session leader's enthusiasm:** When an educator genuinely knows and loves a book, their excitement can motivate the peer tutors to engage more deeply.
- **The book's developmental appropriateness:** Educators should read professional critiques and age-appropriate recommendations to ensure the book is a good fit.

Additional book options for this assignment are listed here.

- *Life Happens Next* (Trueman, 2012), the sequel to *Stuck in Neutral* (Trueman, 2000)
- *Out of My Heart* (Draper, 2021), from the *Out of My Mind* series
- *Out of My Dreams* (Draper, 2024), from the *Out of My Mind* series
- *Petey* (Mikaelsen, 1998)
- *Wonder* (Palacio, 2012)

Approximately two to three weeks prior to the date you intend to hold the discussion, provide students with the novel and the discussion questions. Encourage them to have their responses to each of the questions completed by the date of this training. During the training, the educator can lead a whole-group discussion about the book using their responses to the questions.

Do you ever have peer tutors who encounter challenges with reading and find this assignment too difficult?

Yes. In these cases, you can provide audiobooks, adapted versions of the book, or tutoring sessions.

Do all students need to read the same book?

No. They can, or they can choose from a list you provide.

HOMEWORK

Approximately three weeks before your next training session, assign the class book and discussion questions to each student. Let students know the due date, which should correspond with the day you plan to have your next training session. This is when the class discusses responses for each question as a group. These class discussions tend to be rich, with students sharing great ideas with one another.

The prompt for session five in the reproducible "Digital Portfolio Project" (page 99) is as follows.

> *Please answer the questions about the novel your teacher assigned to you by the due date. Following the class discussion, add any insights you gained from it to your written responses. Then, write one or two paragraphs sharing whether you liked the book, and why or why not. Include in your reflection how the book might apply to you as a peer tutor, to the student you support, or to any other student you know. Upload your written responses to the discussion questions, as well as your reflection, to your digital portfolio.*

SUMMARY

This book talk assignment is often one of the more powerful assignments in this course, as it fosters empathy and an understanding of people in the real world who have needs similar to those of the characters. Peer tutors gain the valuable perspectives of people with disabilities by reading the text and discussing it in groups. Depending on the book and its relevance to the current population of students with disabilities on your campus, this assignment can positively influence how students with disabilities are portrayed and treated.

STUCK IN NEUTRAL BY TERRY TRUEMAN

Name: ______________________________ Period: ____________

Directions: Please read the following quotes from Trueman's (2000) *Stuck in Neutral*. In the space provided, share what these quotes make you think about or feel. How did they apply to Shawn? Feel free to share your personal experiences. Write as much as necessary to make your point.

"I am in here, I'm just sort of stuck in neutral." (page 11)

"My mom, Lindy, still talks to me as if I were a newborn baby or an idiot." (page 11)

"Why educate the uneducable?" (page 45)

"What if somehow, someway, I could get somebody to love me and know me? What if there is a way that I could let somebody know that I am smart and that I like my life and that I don't want to die!" (page 60)

"Will anyone ever know that my life, once lived and then over, was one perfect of remembering? No one will know. No one will know me. I'm just not ready to give up the hope that someday I might be known. I'm not ready." (page 100)

Directions: Reply to the following prompts about the book. Please write a minimum of two sentences to answer each question.

What special ability does Shawn have that no one knows about? (chapter 1)

What is very frustrating for Shawn, especially because he is very smart? (chapter 2)

What did Shawn's dad finally realize after the incident with the crow? (chapter 4)

How do you think Shawn felt at the "big premier" of his father's reading? (chapter 5)

Describe Shawn's seizures. (chapter 6)

What did you learn about Shawn's father and his feelings about Shawn's disability, based on his visit to the classroom? (chapter 7)

Describe the emotions that Shawn is capable of having but no one is aware that he has. (chapter 9)

Why do you think that Cindy and Paul have mixed emotions about appearing on the show with their father? (chapter 10)

What was your reaction to Earl Detraux's side of the story? (chapter 11)

The scene with the boys in chapter 12 is quite violent. Why do you think that the author included this violent episode in the story? (chapter 12)

Describe Shawn's father's actions when he was trying to put Shawn on the ride. Why was he acting that way? (chapter 13)

What was Shawn's dream about? (chapter 14)

What is so different about Shawn's father staying overnight with him, and why is Shawn nervous? (chapter 15)

What do you think happens at the end of the story? (chapter 16)

Considering some of the things that Shawn found frustrating and the information you have learned as a peer tutor, what recommendations do you have for Shawn's family or teachers that might make a positive difference for Shawn?

Reference

Trueman, T. (2000). *Stuck in neutral.* HarperCollins.

OUT OF MY MIND BY SHARON M. DRAPER

Name: ______________________________________ Period: _______________

Please note that *Out of My Mind* was published in 2010, and some of the words used in the book are no longer considered acceptable. For example, even though the word *retarded* was considered wrong to describe a person when the book was written, it was included in this book for emotional effect. We now completely avoid saying this word altogether.

Directions: Reply to the following questions about the book. Please write a minimum of two sentences to answer each question.

Who is Melody?

Who is Penny?

Who is Mrs. V?

What does *inclusion* mean? What do you think about the class that was described as an "inclusion class"?

What can you tell us about Melody's teachers since she began school?

What are Melody's frustrations before getting the communicator device?

What are Melody's frustrations after getting the communicator device?

Have you ever thought about accessibility before? What does it mean to be wheelchair accessible? What other accessibility barriers come up in this book?

Have there been times in your life when you felt excluded? How did they make you feel? Were they similar to what Melody described?

How did Melody change from the beginning of the book to the end?

How did the reporters tell the story of the winning quiz team? How might you have felt if you were Melody? How would you have felt if you were one of the other members of the team?

Toward the end of the book, there is a really intense scene in the car where Melody tries to alert her mom that Penny is behind the car. Melody's mother slaps Penny's leg. How did that scene make you feel?

Describe Melody's feelings before the trip to the airport, while she is there, and after she gets home. How would you have coped with the same situation if you were Melody? If you were one of her teammates? If you were her teacher?

In this story, Melody is very intelligent. How might her story have been different if she were of more average intelligence?

Did this book change your perceptions or views on people with disabilities?

Source: Adapted from Disability Equality in Education. (n.d.). Out of My Mind: Book discussion guide. Author. Accessed at https://static1.squarespace.com/static/60f1a003db93e97a76159740/t/618c3720d6f02b38b8e43d81/1636579105463/Out+of+My+Mind+-+Book+Discussion+Guide.pdf on October 7, 2025.

Reference

Draper, S. M. (2010). *Out of my mind.* Atheneum Books for Young Readers.

CHAPTER 9

Session Six: Research Project

Being a peer tutor has made me consider a career in working with children with autism and their families.

—Peer tutor

By this point, peer tutors will be familiar with many issues affecting people with disabilities, particularly in educational settings. They will likely have developed an interest in at least one area, such as a specific disability, or in broader topics, like assistive technology. This assignment gives students the opportunity to pursue these interests with the added value of strengthening their research and writing skills. In addition, this assignment has the potential to strengthen their skills as a peer tutor, directly benefiting the student they support.

The student learning objective for session six: Students will learn more about a topic of interest that relates to the work they are doing in this class, will gain experience conducting research, and will have an opportunity to enhance their writing skills.

You will need the following materials.

- Access to computers or Chromebooks
- School library time (if possible)
- Reproducible "Research Project" (page 153)
- Reproducible "Research Project Rubric" (page 154)

RESEARCH PROJECT

You can cover this lesson at any time. However, we recommend assigning it near the end of the course. When planning dates for all the training sessions, keep in mind that both the research project and the book talk are more time consuming than other assignments. It might be helpful to have ample time between the two.

Provide each student with a copy of the reproducibles "Research Project" (page 153) and "Research Project Rubric" (page 154). Inform students that this assignment allows them to choose what they want to research and that it should be something of interest to them.

The following list offers possible topics; they are also on the reproducible. This list includes many specific disabilities and some broader topics, such as inclusion and assistive technology. If a student has something else in mind, use discretion about whether their chosen topic would make a good research project.

- Assistive technology
- Attention deficit hyperactivity disorder (ADHD)
- Autism spectrum disorder
- Cerebral palsy
- Disability justice
- Down syndrome
- Dyslexia
- Hearing impairment
- Inclusive education
- Intellectual disabilities
- Universal Design for Learning (UDL)
- Vision impairment
- Vocational opportunities for people with intellectual disabilities

After introducing the assignment and giving students an opportunity to choose their topic, provide the remaining class period to work on their projects. It is ideal to collaborate with the school librarian on this assignment. Some students will undoubtedly require more direction and support than others, and assistance from other school staff members can be helpful, especially those who are familiar with conducting research.

Per the rubric, the projects should be between two to three pages long and include citations for any sources. These sources can include academic journal articles, books, and other similar resources. The project should contain the following components.

- **Introduction:** Identification of the topic and the reason they chose it
- **Description:** A detailed description of the topic, including current research in that area
- **Reflection:** Three to five facts about the topic that they found especially interesting and why
- **Resources:** A discussion of the resources available that are associated with the topic
- **Impact:** A discussion of how this research might help or affect someone else, as well as how it shaped their perspective or altered their understanding of the topic, if applicable

Do some peer tutors struggle to complete this research? If so, do you provide an accommodation or alternative assignments?

Yes. Some peer tutors may have difficulty with researching and writing. Because we view this assignment as such an amazing growth opportunity for peer tutors, we do all that we can to support them, including after-school tutoring and paring down the assignment if needed. Consider alternative assignments, such as changing the format to a slideshow presentation instead of a written report. And, of course, we fully honor any accommodations peer tutors receive through an IEP or 504 plan.

Can more than one peer tutor research the same topic?

Yes. Multiple peer tutors researching the same topics could bring different perspectives. However, while collaboration is always encouraged, it is important to ensure that each student completes their final product individually.

HOMEWORK

Following the class session in which students begin their research with your guidance, students should complete the project by the assigned date and upload it to their digital portfolios. The prompt listed on their handout for session six training is as follows.

Following the prompts on the handout "Research Project," compose a two- or three-page report related to the work you are doing in this class. Once complete, upload the project to your portfolio.

SUMMARY

Although this is a larger and more time-consuming assignment than the others in the course, its benefits are significant. Peer tutors become more skilled in their role and more knowledgeable about issues related to disability and education. In addition, it allows peer tutors to explore their interests while developing and refining valuable research and writing skills. These skills could help prepare students for completing assignments in other classes, as well as the demands of higher education, if that is their chosen path.

RESEARCH PROJECT

The finished research product should be a two- or three-page paper (including citations for any sources you use in your research, such as journal articles or books). Submit your paper to your instructor by the due date: ___________.

This assignment provides you the opportunity to research a topic of your choice. Your topic should be related to the work you are doing in this class. It could be a specific disability or a topic in this field that interests you. Some possible topics follow. If you think of something not on this list, get approval from your teacher.

Follow these instructions.

1. Choose one topic from the following list. (Feel free to choose another topic, if approved by your instructor.)
    - Assistive technology
    - Attention deficit hyperactivity disorder (ADHD)
    - Autism spectrum disorder
    - Cerebral palsy
    - Disability justice
    - Down syndrome
    - Dyslexia
    - Hearing impairment
    - Inclusive education
    - Intellectual disabilities
    - Universal Design for Learning (UDL)
    - Vision impairment
    - Vocational opportunities for people with intellectual disabilities
2. Conduct research on the topic you selected. Your research project should include the following elements.
    - *Introduction*—Identify your topic and explain why you chose it.
    - *Description*—Using reliable resources, provide a detailed description of your topic, including current research (within five years) in that area.
    - *Reflection*—Share three to five facts about this topic that you found especially interesting and why.
    - *Resources*—Share at least three resources (websites, organizations, and the like) related to your topic that could be useful to others.
    - *Impact*—Reflect on and share how this research might help someone else. What did you learn from this research? Did it change your perspective on the topic? If so, how?

RESEARCH PROJECT RUBRIC

This rubric shows the criteria for your research papers. Use this to guide your writing, making sure to address all the report elements listed in the column on the left. As a reminder, sources for this project can include academic journal articles, books, and other similar resources.

Student name: ______________________________ Date: ______________

Report Elements	Performance Criteria	Comments	Points Earned
Chosen topic	Appropriate choice of topic, either selected from the list or approved by the instructor (1 point)		
Introduction	Identification of topic (1 point) Explanation for why you chose the topic (2 points)		
Description	Reliable resources (1 point) Detailed description of topic (2 points) Current research (within 5 years; 1 point)		

Reflection	Three to five interesting facts about the topic (3 points) Reasons why these facts were interesting to you (2 points)		
Resources	Three available resources about the topic (3 points)		
Impact	Ways this research might be helpful to others (1 point) Knowledge you gained and changes in your perspective (2 points)		
Finished product	Two to three pages in length (1 point) Citations for sources (1 point) Completion on or before the due date (1 point) Well-organized information (1 point) In-depth research and reflection (1 point) Correct grammar, spelling, and punctuation (1 point)		
Total:			

page 2 of 2

CHAPTER 10

Session Seven: Digital Portfolio Presentations

At this point in the training sessions, students have reached the point where they can celebrate their experiences as peer tutors. Throughout the course, they have worked very hard to compile their portfolios, which include responses to prompts from all training sessions, personal reflections, and additional entries that demonstrate positive growth for either themselves or the student they worked with. As they present their portfolios to the teacher and their classmates, a strong sense of pride and joy is evident. This sense comes from presenting a well-polished product, teaching and connecting with another person, and knowing they have made a positive difference in someone else's life.

As a result of being a peer tutor, I chose a career in working with people with disabilities.

—Peer tutor

The student learning objective for session seven: By completing the portfolio assignment over the duration of the course, students will learn how to create a digital portfolio showcasing the skills, knowledge, and outcomes they have attained. In addition, students will gain the skills to become effective and confident presenters and adept listeners, as well as valuable insights from the experiences shared by fellow peer tutors.

PRESENTATIONS

Near the end of the course offering, hold a session in which students can present their digital portfolios to the class. Their completed portfolios should include all their responses to prompts and assignments, including the last two prompts (Final Reflection and Additional Entries) on the reproducible "Digital Portfolio Project" (page 99).

The Final Reflection prompt listed on students' handout for session seven training is as follows.

> *Please write at least two paragraphs describing your experiences as a peer tutor and the ways peer tutoring has affected you. Include positive experiences you and the student you supported had, as well as any challenges that you may have experienced.*

The Additional Entries section of the digital portfolio project is updated throughout the course. The prompt listed on students' handout for session seven training is as follows.

> *Please provide at least five additional entries in this section. As mentioned in the second paragraph of this handout, these additions could include student work samples, copies of class projects, photographs of projects the student completed with your support, photographs of the student participating in class activities, positive notes from educators or staff, positive comments other students made, or any other materials that add value to your project. Please be sure to check with teachers to confirm the appropriateness of any entries not listed here. When uploading photographs or work samples, please provide a short note describing what they highlight.*

The presentation of portfolios is a wonderful learning experience for all students. They learn from one another and experience great pride in having created a professional project such as this. The tutored student also experiences great pride as they see and hear about the growth their peer tutor experienced. Peer tutors can also use these digital portfolios to showcase their work as they prepare for college or careers after high school, or even as part of applications for scholarships. Of course, if the peer tutor plans to showcase their portfolio in this manner, they will need to get written permission from the family of the student they supported.

The final assessment of a student's peer tutor portfolio and presentation is based on a forty-point rubric, which is shared in the reproducible "Digital Portfolio Project Rubric" (page 102). The first three sections of the rubric evaluate the required components of the portfolio as outlined in the project description, as well as the overall appearance of the portfolio. Because students complete this portfolio over the duration of the course, feedback is provided long before the final assessment. Teachers see most sections of the portfolio on the due dates following each training session and can offer suggestions for improvement at those times. This ongoing feedback increases the likelihood that students will produce a high-quality final product. The last section of the rubric assesses students' presentation skills, with a focus on eye contact, volume, and pace.

Should peer tutors have training prior to the first day of class?

Although training peer tutors prior to their first day of the semester working with students would be ideal, this is not usually feasible. The priority is for the students with disabilities to attend their classes, and they often need support to do this. Therefore, students are quickly paired with peer tutors after completing the survey, and the peer tutor is given a brief introduction to the needs of the student they will be supporting. The peer tutors are encouraged to focus on getting to know the student they are assigned to during their first week. Throughout the week, changes are made to pairings as necessary. Soon after the first week, peer tutors receive their first training session. By this time, it becomes more practical for the students with disabilities to attend their class without their peer tutors for one class period.

SUMMARY

This chapter described the presentation of the digital portfolio project. As we mentioned, this assignment can become a joyful experience where peer tutors celebrate their own growth and learning and that of the student they supported. Peer tutors increase their organizational skills by creating digital portfolios and gain valuable public-speaking experience by delivering a presentation to an audience of their peers. They leave with a sense of pride, knowing that they made a meaningful difference in the life of another student on their campus. In addition, the successes of the tutored student are highlighted in a portfolio. This assignment is truly a win for everyone involved!

CHAPTER 11
Other Learning Options

While there is tremendous value in holding formal training sessions like those in previous chapters, doing so is not conducive to all school structures and logistics. These training sessions and assignments are simply one way to provide students with opportunities to learn and improve in their role as a peer tutor. However, each school is different, and educators should adapt these training sessions and assignments as needed.

Not only is it important for educators to be flexible with how and when they train peer tutors, it is equally important for educators to teach peer tutors the value of flexibility in their own roles. Whether they are trying to help someone understand an academic task, address life challenges, or interact with others, flexibility is essential. Being adaptable allows both educators and peer tutors to effectively respond in different situations, making them more impactful in their roles.

An alternative to holding formal training sessions is to provide students with assignments that they can independently complete for homework. In addition to the activities in the training sessions in part 2, assign any activities that address your school's needs. Figure 11.1 (page 162) offers a list of sample assignments that you can give to peer tutors.

It may also be the case that assigning *any* class work in addition to their duties as a peer tutor is not appropriate. This is perfectly acceptable as well. Clearly, a peer tutor's most important responsibility is the daily support they provide to their student. The criteria for their grade can be solely based on that. In addition, the one-to-one interactions that occur daily between the educators and the peer tutor allow for just-in-time training. During these moments, educators guide peer tutors on how to implement strategies that will help them provide the best possible assistance to the student they support. This guidance can come from the general

Possible peer tutoring course activities for students in place of formal training sessions are as follows.

Ideal classroom description: Write a description of the ideal inclusive classroom. Include descriptions of the educator's teaching style, the actions and attitudes of the other students, the ways students could support one another, and anything else that you believe would contribute to an inclusive culture in the classroom.

News article critique: Summarize and critique a current news article related to disabilities or special education.

Interview and reflection: Interview an educator or a student about a topic related to inclusive education. Compile a list of five questions addressing what you want to learn, and get approval from your teacher prior to conducting the interview. Share the interview responses as well as what you learned (minimum one page, double spaced).

Research paper: Research specific topics in inclusive education or a related area. Provide findings in the form of an essay or slideshow.

Career exploration: Research employment opportunities related to supporting individuals with disabilities, such as special education instruction, speech-language pathology, occupational therapy, physical therapy, mobility services, vision services, deaf and hard-of-hearing services, adapted physical education, vocational counseling, and independent-living services.

Accessibility survey: Review the accessibility of our school campus or another public area for people with disabilities and provide an action plan for improving or eliminating barriers found.

Universal Design for Learning: Research the principles of Universal Design for Learning. Reflect on how UDL is currently implemented in your classrooms, giving specific examples. Then, provide ideas for how it could be used more (minimum one page, double spaced).

Summary of experience: Write a summary of the positive aspects of all students—including students with disabilities—being taught together in general education classes. Recommend what schools should do to improve student outcomes. Be specific about what the school and the people in it can do to make it happen.

Disability awareness: Choose a children's disability-awareness book and develop an activity related to the book. Read the book and conduct your activity with a group of children. Summarize the book and activity, as well as the children's responses to the activity. There are numerous books written for this purpose. Choose one that piques your interests. Here are a few possible titles: *All My Stripes: A Story for Children With Autism* (Rudolph & Royer, 2015); *Different Just Like Me* (Mitchell, 1999); and *Just Ask! Be Different, Be Brave, Be You* (Sotomayor, 2019).

Movie critique: Select and watch a movie that includes a major character with a disability. Write a reflection about the movie and explain how the character with the disability was portrayed and treated. Did the film have a lasting impact on you? Why or why not? Here are just a few of the many possible movies for this assignment: *The Diving Bell and the Butterfly* (Schnabel, 2007); *Wonder* (Chbosky, 2017); and *The Reason I Jump* (Rothwell, 2020).

Figure 11.1: *Sample assignments.*

Visit ***go.SolutionTree.com/specialneeds*** *for a free reproducible version of this figure.*

educator in the classroom or from the special educator at times when they interact with the peer tutor (such as during the attendance check-in described on page 66). Therefore, it is possible to choose not to do formal training sessions or assignments. Each school must do what is right for its circumstances.

Whatever your course may look like, it is important to provide your students with an adequate balance of work and responsibility. Take care not to overload students with so many assignments that it takes away from their most important role, which is to support a fellow classmate. It is important that peer tutors are provided with the opportunity to learn and to demonstrate responsibility. Students enjoy assuming responsibility for the work they do with the student they support, and they take pride in knowing that they had something to do with the successes of another student.

[Since peer tutoring], I now judge others far less and if I was the manager of a company and a person with a disability applied, I would not hesitate to hire them or find a way to support them so they could work there.

—Peer tutor

SUMMARY

While it may be ideal for schools to offer the formal training sessions described in part 2 of this book, this final chapter presents alternative approaches for training peer tutors, and all are valid. Each school is unique and should do what is right for its current needs and circumstances. What is most important is that peer tutors are monitored and receive many opportunities to learn and improve in their role. These opportunities may involve brief just-in-time training, homework assignments designed to expand their understanding of disability and education, or a combination of methods. If peer tutors are supported in their learning and growth, the outcome is a success.

Epilogue

High school teachers spend their days in the world of adolescents, where students arrive with a host of experiences and knowledge. Educators play a critical role in developing the academic, psychological, social, and emotional identities of young people. Their responsibility is to craft as many experiences as they can that allow students to become the young adults they aspire to be. A critical aspect of this development is broadening the world for each student. To understand who they are as individuals, they must learn about the people in their school community and in the larger world outside school.

A key component in young adults' development is their learning how to support and rely on others. While many adolescents view dependence as a sign of weakness, educators know that interdependence and the ability to work with others are essential to personal and professional success. Peer tutoring support systems are one way to foster and develop these skills in students.

Implementing a peer tutoring course involves multiple steps. The reproducible "Peer Tutoring Course Action Plan" (page 166) can be a helpful tool during the initial development phase; however, challenges and barriers are inevitable, as they are with any new course. With thoughtful planning, creativity, and determination, most obstacles can be successfully overcome, and schools can reap the benefits.

Among the many benefits outlined in this book is the ability of peer tutoring to provide one-to-one support for students with disabilities in general education classrooms. Because it is neither practical nor desirable to provide adult support in every situation where assistance is needed, it just makes sense to engage the abundance of peers available in schools. Peer tutors provide much-needed support for inclusive education and thereby foster a school culture that values diversity. As a result, students carry with them greater acceptance and appreciation of human differences, helping shape a more inclusive society in the future.

PEER TUTORING COURSE ACTION PLAN

Use this action plan to outline the steps needed to develop and implement a peer tutoring course, highlighting who is responsible for each action. The intended outcome is a comprehensive plan for all members of the peer tutoring course creation team to follow.

Step to Take	Action to Take	Person Responsible	Projected Completion Date	Actual Completion Date	Follow-Up Plan (if needed)

References and Resources

ADA National Network. (n.d.). *What is the definition of disability under the ADA?* Accessed at https://adata.org/faq/what-definition-disability-under-ada on February 19, 2026.

Agran, M., Jackson, L., Kurth, J. A., Ryndak, D., Burnette, K., Jameson, M., et al. (2020). Why aren't students with severe disabilities being placed in general education classrooms: Examining the relations among classroom placement, learner outcomes, and other factors. *Research and Practice for Persons With Severe Disabilities, 45*(1), 4–13.

American Network of Community Options and Resources. (2025). *The state of America's direct support workforce crisis 2025.* Author. Accessed at www.ancor.org/wp-content/uploads/2025/10/The-State-of-Americas-Direct-Support-Workforce-Crisis-2025.pdf on February 25, 2026.

Aristotle. (1886). *The Nicomachean ethics* (3rd ed.; F. H. Peters, Trans.). Kegan Paul, Trench. (Original work published ca. 340 B.C.E.)

Audley, S., & Jović, S. (2020). Making meaning of children's social interactions: The value tensions among school, classroom, and peer culture. *Learning, Culture and Social Interaction, 24*, Article 100357.

Bal, P. M., & Veltkamp, M. (2013). How does fiction reading influence empathy? An experimental investigation on the role of emotional transportation. *PLoS One, 8*(1), Article e55341.

Bauby, J.-D. (1998). *The diving bell and the butterfly: A memoir of life in death.* Vintage International.

Biggs, E. E., Carter, E. W., & Gustafson, J. (2017). Efficacy of peer support arrangements to increase peer interaction and AAC use. *American Journal on Intellectual and Developmental Disabilities, 122*(1), 25–48.

Bond, R. J. (2001). *Peer tutors of students with moderate and severe disabilities in general education high school settings* [Unpublished master's thesis]. San Diego State University.

Bond, R. J., & Castagnera, E. (2006). Peer supports and inclusive education: An underutilized resource. *Theory Into Practice, 45*(3), 224–229.

Boroditsky, L. (2011, February 1). How language shapes thought. *Scientific American.* Accessed at www.scientificamerican.com/article/how-language-shapes-thought on February 22, 2026.

Brass, N. R., Hung, C., Stephen, T., Bergin, C., Rose, C., & Prewett, S. (2024). Student's and classmates' prosocial behavior predict academic engagement in middle school. *Journal of Youth and Adolescence, 53*(12), 2789–2800.

Brock, M. E., & Huber, H. B. (2017). Are peer support arrangements an evidence-based practice? A systematic review. *The Journal of Special Education, 51*(3), 150–163. https://doi.org/10.1177/0022466917708184

Broer, S. M., Doyle, M. B., & Giangreco, M. F. (2005). Perspectives of students with intellectual disabilities about their experiences with paraprofessional support. *Exceptional Children, 71*(4), 415–430.

Brooks, R. J. (2014). *Exploring the long-term benefits from peer tutoring high school students with significant disabilities* [Doctoral dissertation, Claremont Graduate University]. ProQuest Dissertations and Theses. www.proquest.com/openview/03988e78b57e5b88a0c4c482eb3bc2ef/1.pdf?pq-origsite=gscholar&cbl=18750

Brooks, R. J., & Castagnera, E. (2010). *Peer tutoring and support: Making inclusive education work.* PEAK Parent Center.

Carter, E. W., Asmus, J., Moss, C. K., Biggs, E. E., Bolt, D. M., Born, T. L., et al. (2016). Randomized evaluation of peer support arrangements to support the inclusion of high school students with severe disabilities. *Exceptional Children, 82*(2), 209–233.

Carter, E. W., Gustafson, J. R., Sreckovic, M. A., Steinbrenner, J. R. D., Pierce, N. P., Bord, A., et al. (2017). Efficacy of peer support interventions in general education classrooms for high school students with autism spectrum disorder. *Remedial and Special Education, 38*(4), 207–221. https://doi.org/10.1177/0741932516672067

Carter, E. W., Sisco, L. G., Melekoglu, M. A., & Kurkowski, C. (2007). Peer supports as an alternative to individually assigned paraprofessionals in inclusive high school classrooms. *Research and Practice for Persons With Severe Disabilities, 32*(4), 213–227.

Carter, E. W., Steinbrenner, J. R. D., & Hall, L. J. (2019). Exploring feasibility and fit: Peer-mediated interventions for high school students with autism spectrum disorders. *School Psychology Review, 48*(2), 157–169. https://doi.org/10.17105/SPR-2017-0112.V48-2

Castagnera, E., Fisher, D., Rodifer, K., Sax, C., & Frey, N. (2003). *Deciding what to teach and how to teach it: Connecting students through curriculum and instruction* (2nd ed.). PEAK Parent Center.

The Center on Secondary Education for Students with Autism Spectrum Disorder. (n.d.). *Peer supports facilitator manual.* Author. Accessed at https://csesa.fpg.unc.edu/sites/csesa.fpg.unc.edu/files/Peer%20Supports%20Manual.pdf on October 7, 2025.

Chbosky, S. (Director). (2017). *Wonder* [Film]. Participant Media; Walden Media; Mandeville Films; TIK Films.

Collins, B. C., Lo, Y.-Y., Haughney, K., & Park, G. (2021). Using peer-delivered simultaneous prompting to teach health content to students with moderate intellectual disability. *Education and Training in Autism and Developmental Disabilities, 56*(3), 293–305. https://doi.org/10.1177/215416472105600305

Cushing, L. S., & Kennedy, C. H. (1997). Academic effects of providing peer support in general education classrooms on students without disabilities. *Journal of Applied Behavior Analysis, 30*(1), 139–151. https://doi.org/10.1901/jaba.1997.30-139

Disability Equality in Education. (n.d.). Out of My Mind: *Book discussion guide.* Author. Accessed at https://static1.squarespace.com/static/60f1a003db93e97a76159740/t/618c3720d6f02b38b8e43d81/1636579105463/Out+of+My+Mind+-+Book+Discussion+Guide.pdf on October 7, 2025.

Downing, J. E., Hanreddy, A., & Peckham-Hardin, K. D. (2015). *Teaching communication skills to students with severe disabilities* (3rd ed.). Brookes.

Draper, S. M. (2010). *Out of my mind.* Atheneum Books for Young Readers.

Draper, S. M. (2021). *Out of my heart.* Atheneum Books for Young Readers.

Draper, S. M. (2024). *Out of my dreams.* Atheneum Books for Young Readers.

Falvey, M. A., Forest, M., Pearpoint, J., & Rosenberg, R. L. (2002). Building connections. In J. S. Thousand, R. A. Villa, & A. I. Nevin (Eds.), *Creativity and collaborative learning: The practical guide to empowering students, teachers, and families* (2nd ed.; pp. 29–54). Brookes.

Family Educational Rights and Privacy Act, 20 U.S.C. § 1232g (1974).

Fernández-Batanero, J. M., Montenegro-Rueda, M., Fernández-Cerero, J., & García-Martínez, I. (2022). Assistive technology for the inclusion of students with disabilities: A systematic review. *Educational Technology Research and Development, 70*(5), 1911–1930. https://doi.org/10.1007/s11423-022-10127-7

Gee, K., Ryndak, D. L., Fisher, M., & Walker, V. L. (2024). Access to the general education curriculum for students with extensive support needs: Experts' perspectives. *Research and Practice for Persons With Severe Disabilities, 49*(1), 3–19. https://doi.org/10.1177/15407969231219027

Haas, A., Vannest, K. J., Fuller, M. C., & Ganz, J. B. (2022). Understanding the effect size of peer-mediated academic instruction: A meta-analysis. *Focus on Autism and Other Developmental Disabilities, 37*(1), 3–12. https://doi.org/10.1177/10883576211023329

Handicap. (n.d.). In *Merriam-Webster's online dictionary*. Accessed at www.merriam-webster.com/dictionary/handicap on March 2, 2026.

Hehir, T., Grindal, T., Freeman, B., Lamoreau, R., Borquaye, Y., & Burke, S. (2016, August). *A summary of the evidence on inclusive education*. Abt Associates. Accessed at https://alana.org.br/wp-content/uploads/2016/12/A_Summary_of_the_evidence_on_inclusive_education.pdf on November 16, 2025.

Higashida, N. (2016). *The reason I jump: The inner voice of a thirteen-year-old boy with autism* (K. Yoshida & D. Mitchell, Trans.). Random House.

Huber, H. B., & Carter, E. W. (2023). Impact and individualization of peer support arrangements for high school students with autism using structural analysis. *Inclusion, 11*(1), 1–22. https://doi.org/10.1352/2326-6988-11.1.1

Individuals With Disabilities Education Act Amendments of 1997, Pub. L. No. 105-17, 111 Stat. 37 (1997).

Individuals With Disabilities Education Improvement Act of 2004, Pub. L. No. 108-446 § 300.115 (2004).

KARE 11. (2018, November 1). *Land of 10,000 Stories: 2nd grade friendship binds HS honor student, teen with autism* [Video file]. Accessed at www.youtube.com/watch?v=GwKvTPTIUME on February 22, 2026.

Katz, L., Sax, C., & Fisher, D. (2003). *Activities for a diverse classroom: Connecting students* (2nd ed.). PEAK Parent Center.

Klavina, A., & Block, M. E. (2008). The effect of peer tutoring on interaction behaviors in inclusive physical education. *Adapted Physical Activity Quarterly, 25*(2), 132–158. https://doi.org/10.1123/apaq.25.2.132

Longwill, A. W., & Kleinert, H. L. (1998). The unexpected benefits of high school peer tutoring. *TEACHING Exceptional Children, 30*(4), 60–65.

Mahoney, M. W. M. (2023). Peer-mediated instruction and intervention to support the academic achievement of secondary students with autism spectrum disorder: A systematic review of the literature. *The Journal of Special Education Apprenticeship, 12*(1). https://doi.org/10.58729/2167-3454.1159

Malone, K. W., Fodor, J. A., & Hollingshead, A. (2019). Peer tutoring to support inclusion of students with the most significant cognitive disabilities at the secondary level. *Inclusion, 7*(1), 1–11. https://doi.org/10.1352/2326-6988-7.1.1

Mar, R. A., Oatley, K., Hirsh, J., dela Paz, J., & Peterson, J. B. (2006). Bookworms versus nerds: Exposure to fiction versus non-fiction, divergent associations with social ability, and the simulation of fictional social worlds. *Journal of Research in Personality, 40*(5), 694–712.

Maryland Coalition for Inclusive Education. (2025, February 27). *Peer tutoring: A key to inclusive education success* [Video file]. Accessed at www.youtube.com/watch?v=afczWFjyLDs on February 20, 2026.

Mauer, E., & Swanson, E. (2025). Cross-age peer tutoring to improve literacy outcomes for students with disabilities. *TEACHING Exceptional Children, 57*(4), 286–293. https://doi.org/10.1177/00400599241231229

Mauri, C., Radetski, K., & Wong, A. (1995). *Exceptional programs department: Peer tutor training manual* [Unpublished manuscript]. San Diego City Schools.

Mikaelsen, B. (1998). *Petey*. Hyperion Books for Children.

Mitchell, L. (1999). *Different just like me*. Charlesbridge.

Morelli, S. A., Lieberman, M. D., & Zaki, J. (2015). The emerging study of positive empathy. *Social and Personality Psychology Compass, 9*(2), 57–68.

Morgan, G. A., Kim, J. Y., & Fienup, D. M. (2020). Effects of nonreciprocal peer tutoring with preschool students. *Behavior Analysis in Practice, 13*(4), 950–954. https://doi.org/10.1007/s40617-020-00422-1

Owen-DeSchryver, J., Ziegler, M., Matthews, A., Mayberry, M., & Carter, E. (2024). The reciprocity of peer-mediated interventions: Examining outcomes for peers. *School Psychology Review, 53*(3), 223–235. https://doi.org/10.1080/2372966X.2022.2039959

Palacio, R. J. (2012). *Wonder*. Knopf.

Pineda Zapata, Y., & Brooks, R. (2017). *Adapting unstoppable learning* (D. Fisher & N. Frey, Eds.). Solution Tree Press.

Pinto, P., Simpson, C., & Bakken, J. P. (2009). Research-based instructions to increase communication skills for students with disabilities. *International Journal of Special Education, 24*(3), 99–109.

Rahman, M. A. (2025). Psychosocial stressors and determinants of loneliness among school-going adolescents globally. *Journal of Affective Disorders, 378*, 201–210. https://doi.org/10.1016/j.jad.2025.02.093

Riess, H. (2017). The science of empathy. *Journal of Patient Experience, 4*(2), 74–77. https://doi.org/10.1177/2374373517699267

Rothwell, J. (Director). (2020). *The reason I jump* [Film]. MetFilm Production; Runaway Fridge Productions; Vulcan Productions; The British Film Institute.

Roza, S. A., & Guimarães, S. R. K. (2022). The relationship between reading and empathy: An integrative literature review. *Psicologia: Teoria e Prática, 24*(2), Article ePTPPE14051.

Rudolph, S., & Royer, D. (2015). *All my stripes: A story for children with autism* (J. Zivoin, Illus.). Magination Press.

Sass, E. J. (2015, November 9). *Speaking and writing about people with disabilities* [Blog post]. Accessed at www.eds-resources.com/edpeoplefirst.htm on October 7, 2025.

Schaefer, J. M., Cannella-Malone, H. I., & Carter, E. W. (2016). The place of peers in peer-mediated interventions for students with intellectual disability. *Remedial and Special Education, 37*(6), 345–356. https://doi.org/10.1177/0741932516629220

Schnabel, J. (Director). (2007). *Le scaphandre et le papillon* [The diving bell and the butterfly] [Film]. Pathé Renn Production; Canal+; The Kennedy/Marshall Company; France 3 Cinéma.

Shukla, S., Kennedy, C. H., & Cushing, L. S. (1998). Adult influence on the participation of peers without disabilities in peer support programs. *Journal of Behavioral Education, 8*(4), 397–413.

Shukla, S., Kennedy, C. H., & Cushing, L. S. (1999). Intermediate school students with severe disabilities: Supporting their social participation in general education classrooms. *Journal of Positive Behavior Interventions, 1*(3), 130–140.

Snow, K. (2005). *To ensure inclusion, freedom, and respect for all we must use people first language*. Colorado Department of Education. Accessed at www.cde.state.co.us/sites/default/files/documents/early/downloads/prespedonlinecourses/peoplefirst.pdf on October 7, 2025.

Sotomayor, S. (2019). *Just ask! Be different, be brave, be you* (R. López, Illus.). Philomel Books.

Staub, D., Spaulding, M., Peck, C. A., Gallucci, C., & Schwartz, I. S. (1996). Using nondisabled peers to support the inclusion of students with disabilities at the junior high school level. *Journal of the Association for Persons With Severe Handicaps, 21*(4), 194–205.

Tamir, D. I., Bricker, A. B., Dodell-Feder, D., & Mitchell, J. P. (2015). Reading fiction and reading minds: The role of simulation in the default network. *Social Cognitive and Affective Neuroscience, 11*(2), 215–224.

Thompson, D. E., Jr. (2011). *The perceptions of peer tutoring among middle school teachers within multi-ability classrooms* [Doctoral dissertation, The University of Memphis]. The University of Memphis Digital Commons. https://digitalcommons.memphis.edu/etd/341

Thompson, J. R., Walker, V. L., Snodgrass, M. R., Nelson, J. A., Carpenter, M. E., Hagiwara, M., et al. (2020). Planning supports for students with intellectual disability in general education classrooms. *Inclusion, 8*(1), 27–42. https://doi.org/10.1352/2326-6988-8.1.27

Travers, H. E., & Carter, E. W. (2022a). How do peers benefit from peer-mediated interventions? Examining impact within secondary and postsecondary programs. *Research and Practice for Persons With Severe Disabilities, 47*(2), 72–89. https://doi.org/10.1177/15407969221093380

Travers, H. E., & Carter, E. W. (2022b). A portrait of peers within peer-mediated interventions: A literature review. *Focus on Autism and Other Developmental Disabilities, 37*(2), 71–82. https://doi.org/10.1177/10883576211073698

Travers, H. E., & Carter, E. W. (2022c). A systematic review of how peer-mediated interventions impact students without disabilities. *Remedial and Special Education, 43*(1), 40–57.

Trueman, T. (2000). *Stuck in neutral.* HarperCollins.

Trueman, T. (2012). *Life happens next.* HarperTeen.

University of Minnesota Extension. (n.d.). *Creating community across generations*. Accessed at https://extension.umn.edu/vital-connections/creating-community-across-generations on February 22, 2026.

University of New Hampshire Institute on Disability. (2011, May 5). *Voices of friendship (1996)* [Video file]. Accessed at www.youtube.com/watch?v=g6Yp4MzNQMk on October 8, 2025.

U.S. Commission on Civil Rights. (2025, September). *The federal response to teacher shortage impacts on students with disabilities: A briefing before the United States Commission on Civil Rights held in Washington, DC.* Author. Accessed at www.usccr.gov/files/2025-09/teacher-shortage-report-final.pdf on February 25, 2026.

van der Meulen, K., Granizo, L., & del Barrio, C. (2021). Emotional peer support interventions for students with SEND: A systematic review. *Frontiers in Psychology, 12*, Article 797913. https://doi.org/10.3389/fpsyg.2021.797913

Van Ryzin, M. J., Murray, C., & Roseth, C. J. (2024). The effects of cooperative learning on self-reported peer relations, peer support, and classroom engagement among students with disabilities. *The Journal of Educational Research, 117*(6), 355–364. https://doi.org/10.1080/00220671.2024.2410494

Van Ryzin, M. J., & Roseth, C. J. (2022). The longitudinal relationship between peer relations and empathy and their joint contribution to reducing bullying in middle school: Findings from a randomized trial of cooperative learning. *Journal of Prevention and Health Promotion, 3*(2), 147–165. https://doi.org/10.1177/26320770221094032

Villa, R. A., Thousand, J. S., & Nevin, A. I. (2010). *Collaborating with students in instruction and decision making: The untapped resource.* Corwin.

Villalobos, P. (n.d.). *Peer tutor resource manual* [Unpublished manuscript]. San Diego State University Interwork Institute.

Wang, J., Bettini, E., & Cheyney, K. (2013). Students with emotional and behavioral disorders as peer tutors: A valued role. *Beyond Behavior, 23*(1), 17–24. https://doi.org/10.1177/107429561302300103

Wilt, C. L., & Morningstar, M. E. (2020). Student perspectives on peer mentoring in an inclusive postsecondary education context. *Journal of Inclusive Postsecondary Education, 2*(1). https://doi.org/10.13021/jipe.2020.2461

Watts, G. W., Bryant, D. P., & Carroll, M. L. (2019). Students with emotional-behavioral disorders as cross-age tutors: A synthesis of the literature. *Behavioral Disorders, 44*(3).

Winthrop, R., Shoukry, Y., & Nitkin, D. (2025). *The disengagement gap: Why student engagement isn't what parents expect.* Center for Universal Education at Brookings & Transcend. Accessed at www.brookings.edu/wp-content/uploads/2025/01/REPORT_The-Disengagement-Gap_FINAL.pdf on April 1, 2026.

Index

S

Adapting Unstoppable Learning
Yazmin Pineda Zapata and Rebecca Brooks
The Unstoppable Learning model includes seven elements—planning, launching, consolidating, assessing, adapting, managing, and leading. This practical guide expands upon the adapting element, giving readers a clear path for supporting students with varying needs. A variety of forms, tools, and diagrams are also included.
BKF734

Leading Special Education
Breauna C. Wall
Supporting and empowering special education teachers is essential for student success, as author Breauna C. Wall emphasizes with this guide. She advocates for reform in special education programs, including robust systems of support, mentoring, and ongoing professional development for special education teachers.
BKG247

Reaching Every Learner
Cara Shores
Whether you're a general education teacher or a special education teacher, if you teach students with disabilities, this book is for you. Author Cara Shores provides a three-tiered instructional framework that helps educators establish integral baselines of performance for students, offering strategies for assessment, intervention, and remediation to ensure student growth and mastery learning.
BKG272

The Collaborative IEP
Kristen M. Bordonaro and Megan Clarke
In this guide, discover the essential steps and vital understandings for team members to create student-centered IEPs. This book simplifies the IEP writing process and provides practical strategies and structures that can help all educators create compliant and effective IEPs for students.
BKG122

Solution Tree | Press 

Visit SolutionTree.com or call 800.733.6786 to order.